Advance Praise for
Climbing Down the Ladder

"Laura Black's writing is insightful, raw, and from the heart. The story of how she reached the pinnacle of her career is riveting but it's how she climbed down that offers us unique lessons. *Climbing Down the Ladder* is indispensable in today's world, where there is so much riding on success and pressure to get to the top—but so little advice on how to step down. Laura is the woman to guide and uplift us on our journey with courage, humor, and self-compassion."

—*Robin Silver, Principal, Miles & Stockbridge*

"*Climbing Down the Ladder* is a MUST READ for the millions of women who, after reaching the peak of their professions while balancing family life and the multitude of attendant responsibilities, find themselves asking, 'NOW WHAT?' Black's memoir is insightful, tender, witty, and more than anything else, a gift to those navigating this next stage of life."

—*Emily Rapp Black,* New York Times *bestselling author of* The Still Point of the Turning World

CLIMBING DOWN THE LADDER

A Journey to a Different Kind of Happy

LAURA BLACK

CAZCO PRESS
LCB VENTURES, LLC

To my children and grandchildren—
> Danny, Laura, Andy, Kristin, Jackie, Lorin, Addie, Connor, and Zachary
> Enjoy the climbs my loves, for soon it will all be but a memory.

To my husband—
> Charles, my everything, thank you for holding my hand as we enter new waters.

To my siblings and friends—
> We laugh, cry, and guide one another to safe shores.

Contents

Prologue

AS MY FATHER'S wood-paneled station wagon pulled up to a red light, I pressed my nose against the back window and took in the hospital-like building. The sign hanging on the concrete façade read, "Nursing and Rehabilitation Center." I was eight years old and I had never seen so many vulnerable people all in one place. They looked saggy—used-up and wrinkled like the pads of my fingertips when I got out of the tub. Some were strapped into wheelchairs and parked on the porch, as if they had misbehaved and been put in time-out. Others clung to walkers or were wedged into rocking chairs that were scattered willy-nilly like pick-up sticks. Two younger women, in crisp white nurses' uniforms, stood aloof in a far corner of the manicured grounds. They were smoking cigarettes and laughing, maybe sharing naughty jokes.

I waved my chubby hand at a silver-haired lady wearing a purple caftan and large, gold-hooped earrings. She didn't wave back. Instead, she stared straight ahead, rocking back and forth in rhythm to a silent cadence. Perhaps she was lost in memory, or perhaps she was simply lost.

I was already terrified of quicksand, burglars, and earthquakes; now I added getting old to the list. As the light turned green and my father drove off, I stashed away the image.

It didn't reemerge until, within a few years of one another, I sold my company and my three grown children settled into lives of their own. Up until that point, like a suitcase that wouldn't close, my life had spilled over with purpose. I had built a booming business, raised three children that I was proud of, and juggled the infinite accompanying responsibilities from carpooling to college touring. Suddenly, I had no reason to wake up early to prep for a meeting or stay up late to sniff a teenager's breath for alcohol.

The memory of the people from that nursing home, a personification of purposelessness, emerged from a pocket of fear and jolted me into a frantic search for meaning.

When I ascended the ladder to help build one of the largest temporary legal staffing companies in the country, my goals were quantifiable, measured by market share and bottom-line profitability. Now, climbing down, without aspiration or destination, I had no idea where I was headed or how to tell if I'd arrived. I felt like the container of cottage cheese that had sat too long in my refrigerator and that no one wanted because it was past its "use by" date. Was that it? Were the days of aspiration and achievement simply over? No, I would come to learn, these concepts simply needed to be reframed.

I am not alone. According to the Pew Research Center, in the third quarter of 2020 there were roughly 28.6 million retired baby boomers, a 3.2 million increase over the same quarter in 2019.[*] We are the generation that led the great migration of women into the professions. (The Civil Rights Act of 1964; the creation of the U.S. Equal Employment Opportunity Commission in 1965; and the 1978 Pregnancy Discrimination Act were all instrumental in opening these doors for women.) And in the same way that we lacked role models on the way up, we lack them on the way down.

Our careers provided more than money. They gave us identity through titles and status. We became doctors, lawyers, CEOs, and CFOs. We attended and spoke at conferences, schmoozed with

---

[*] "The pace of Boomer retirements has accelerated in the past year." Pew Research Center, Washington, D.C. (November 9, 2020)

colleagues, exchanged business cards, and asked for referrals. We relished challenge and lauded accomplishment.

We had a ready, enthusiastic answer to "What do you do?"

When we lost our work identities, many of us were left adrift—out to sea without anchors or markers, searching for a new North Star. And with life expectancies longer than ever, we now had decades to fill with new purpose and meaning.

I knew that my fate was not to dwindle or be diminished; I was a person who willingly faced a challenge. However, in order to move forward, I had to first look back and recognize the role that my work identity played in ego-fulfillment, validation, and self-worth. What were the roots of those needs? And what continued to drive them? Was I sentenced to a never-ending search for accomplishment and reinforcement?

I learned that I had been mistakenly seeking new ways to fill old voids. After much digging, I unearthed a different kind of happy, a contentment that was not dependent on what I did or how I looked, but on who I was. This realization was a lifetime in the making: and it was not about ascending another ladder. Instead, it was about relinquishing the need to climb. When that happened, my life was transformed. It was no longer fueled by the search but powered by the present.

PART I

LOOKING BACK
TO GO FORWARD

1

If They Only Knew

TO STEADY MY nerves, I inhaled through my nose, held the breath, and exhaled through my mouth—all to the count of four. As the keynote speaker for a "Woman and Law" seminar, I felt anxious about conveying the rigors of balancing work-life responsibilities in a way that wouldn't alienate vulnerable second-year law students who I knew, from experience, were already feeling overwhelmed.

The professor, Dr. Applefield, a slim, blond, forty-something woman wearing a navy pantsuit from Talbot's, ushered me to a podium set up in the front of a file-folder colored room not much bigger than my bedroom. She introduced me to the audience of fifty students, mostly women, who were dressed in various shades of blue jeans, boots or sneakers, and hoodies or sweaters:

"We are honored to have Laura Black come and speak to us today about women in the legal profession. As you may know, Laura opted out of the traditional legal career trajectory. She is the CEO of one of the largest temporary staffing company in the country. Laura has won numerous awards for her business success including "Maryland's Top 100 Women" and The Girl Scout's "Distinguished Woman" designation. She is the mother of three children, two boys and a girl."

Oy, always such pressure to live up to the build-up.

I thanked Dr. Applefield. Like her, I was in my mid-forties and I, too, wore a suit. Mine, however, was a size 14, black, with an elastic-waist skirt with matching tank top and jacket—all purchased from the plus-size department at Saks. Back then my dark hair was cut short and made straight with a flat iron. I always wore black flats for comfort, minimal jewelry (so as not to appear pretentious), and a designer handbag to indicate that even if I didn't dress in high-fashion, I knew it existed, and I could afford it.

"I'm honored to be here this afternoon," I began. "It wasn't that long ago that I, too, was in law school and anxious about my career. That is, whenever I could focus past my panic over the looming bar exam." When the audience's laughter quieted, I continued with a well-rehearsed speech about the importance of developing the skills and contacts to bring in revenue—also known as rainmaking.

Afterwards, when I asked for questions, a dozen hands shot up. The first few inquiries were routine: big firms versus small firms, the availability of part-time work, and the pros and cons of clerking before practicing. Then I called on a wispy-framed brunette with a short, choppy haircut and jeans that hung low on her hips.

"Can we really have it all?" she asked. Her voice was strained, questioning, but also hopeful. "If so, how do we balance our career goals with all the other responsibilities in our lives?"

I took a sip of water and waited for the whirls of a police siren speeding past the building to subside.

"What kind of responsibilities are you referring to?" I asked her.

"I want to have children and my parents are getting older and growing dependent on me. I like to volunteer, and I need time for exercise and self-care."

The other students leaned forward in their seats, pens in hand, ready to memorialize my advice on yellow legal pads.

I took a deep breath and thought, *the truth—always the truth.*

"Yes, you can do it all—but none of it perfectly."

Once again, laughter.

As they scribbled notes, I talked about the need to prioritize. "You must develop the habit of asking yourself, 'Will this really matter a week or a month from now?' For example, missing a deadline to file a motion will matter. Dirty dishes left in the sink will not. Showing up late to court is not acceptable—to an aerobics class, okay."

What I didn't share—because I didn't yet know it—was the advice to savor these years even in their occasional wildness and anxious uncertainty. There were more rewards in the journey than the destination, I wanted to say. I longed to encourage them to enjoy the climb up that career ladder while the steps were steady and could bear their weight easily. Because, one day, and sooner than later, it would all be but a memory and part of their past. And those same steps would begin to erode and wobble with age; what was secure would begin to feel uncertain.

I took a few more questions about interviewing techniques and résumé building. When Dr. Applefield said, "We're almost out of time, let's have one last question," I called on an older student wearing glasses that were too large for her face.

"You seem so confident," she said. "I'm nervous when I interview for jobs, and I'm scared of the responsibility of advising people. How can I gain confidence? Is it something you're born with, or can it be learned?"

I glanced at my watch. It was time to end.

"It can be acquired," I said.

If they only knew...

2

Half as Beautiful as Mom

I WAS SIX years old the first time I experienced shame. Sitting cross-legged on my parents' king-size bed, I watched as my mother dressed for a gala. She tucked her Jacqueline Kennedy-like hair into a sheer net for protection, dappled foundation on her face, and painted a sea-blue eyeshadow on her eyelids. She wiggled into a girdle and longline bra, then slipped her firm body into a royal blue strapless gown. As she posed in front of her full-length mirror, I gasped. She looked like Cinderella at the Royal Ball.

I then caught my own reflection. The elastic of my pajama bottoms strained over the rolls of my stomach and my face was swollen, like I was trying to blow-up a balloon. My father walked into the bedroom to hurry my mother along. Awestruck, he whispered, "You are magnificent." Then he eyed me up and down and said, "I pray that one day you'll grow up to be half as beautiful as your mother." Mom beamed. I wanted to disappear.

Memories rise from extremes. So perhaps there were moments when my weight did not define me—but I cannot recall any. I can recall wishing I were invisible when the school nurse weighed me in front of the other kids in my physical education class to corroborate the correlation between obesity and failing those 1960's presidential fitness tests.

I tried my hardest, but my arms did not have the strength to lift my bulk to the top of the metal pull-up bar. I did not have the stamina to run around the baseball field in the allotted time, so I walked. And the only push-ups I could manage were the kind that involved ice cream pops. Failing was painful. That others bore witness was humiliating.

I can still see my father's raised eyebrow when I reached into my plastic pumpkin for a piece of Halloween candy. I can still hear my mother say, "You know you don't need that," when I reached for a second slice of birthday cake. For a time, I stopped eating sweets in front of them and instead smuggled the contraband to the safety and peace of my bedroom.

I waited until they were in bed and the house was silent. Then I wrapped my pink, terry-cloth robe over my pajamas, tiptoed into the garage and headed to the extra freezer filled with goodies like frozen cheese danishes, homemade strudel, and chocolate-filled rugelach. I grabbed whatever I thought they wouldn't miss and stuffed it inside my bathrobe sleeve. Back in my room, I downed the goodies as fast as I could, in case my parents came in to check on me.

Appearances mattered. It was the early 1960s, and my parents were South Floridian socialites. They traveled across the globe, hobnobbed with the rich and famous, and hosted lavish extravaganzas attended by the crème de la crème of the sunshine state.

My appearance, because of my weight, was an embarrassment to them. They dragged me to doctors, weight-loss programs, and gyms. They even offered me one thousand dollars if I lost thirty pounds. When nothing else worked, they tried what might be called "tough love."

One humid Miami night, my father planned on taking Mom, my brother Jay, my sister Gail, and me to a fancy dinner with bigshot clients. He was a distinguished businessman, and his clients were prominent and important people. I wanted him to be proud of me, so I put on my best dress, the one my grandmother made by hand from her tenement apartment in New York. It was a pink chiffon shift embossed with matching fuzzy flowers. I wore black patent leather party shoes, even though they pinched my toes. I tamed my frizzy hair with a pink headband that matched my dress.

I held my breath as I walked into the living room where my parents were waiting. Mom had her hair done that afternoon and wore a new red suit and heels dyed to match. Dad, six feet tall with a receding hairline, looked spiffy in a charcoal gray suit, white shirt, and a wide red tie—to coordinate perfectly with Mom.

"Hi, Daddy," I said, praying for an *Oh, you look so beautiful* in response.

Instead, he looked me over, shook his head and said, "I'm sorry, I can't take you with us tonight. You're going to have to stay home."

"Why?"

"You're too fat—it's embarrassing. Why don't you work on losing some weight and then maybe next time you can come."

I looked to my mother. Silence.

I felt crushed—like the grapes that Lucy and Ethel stomped into pulp on one of my favorite episodes of *I Love Lucy*.

It's not that I didn't try to lose weight. I could rattle off the calorie counts of most foods before I learned the names of the planets: a glazed doughnut had 270 calories; a vanilla milkshake, 500; and two pancakes with maple syrup and butter, 670.

I tried to stay away from these high-calorie foods, but most days I gave up by dinner. Diets demanded deprivation—how does one deny a hungry soul? Sara Lee, Betty Crocker, and Little Debbie triumphed.

I was a ballerina too heavy to balance on toes. A swimmer prone to ear infections. A tennis player who couldn't master a forehand, backhand, or serve. Exercise was not for me. I was a thinker, a reader. I devoured Carolyn Haywood and Beverly Cleary novels, losing myself in the antics of Betsy and Eddie or Beezus and Ramona. Frustrated, my mother would announce, "Enough with the reading. Get outside and move your body, burn some calories."

Lost in a "you can never be too thin or too rich" culture, I acted out and crossed boundaries for morsels of validation. I even pulled my mother's copy of Dr. Spock off the shelf to try and understand what was wrong with me. I read advice like, "children should be hugged" and "they need to hear that they are special." My parents must have skipped over those chapters, or perhaps they simply weren't interested.

I longed for a confidante, a friend or grownup, to cradle my sadness and soothe it to sleep. Instead, I turned to the Royal Typewriter in our den and with my pointer fingers, key by key, I pecked my pain.

A long look in the mirror painfully reveals how the outside sees you
Not how your inside feels.
Inside you felt happy—light and full of cheer
Then that long, last look—could that be you that's there.

MY FATHER KEPT his favorite picture of my mother on his night table in a five-by-eight-inch, Jay Strongwater frame. It was taken when she was in her early twenties. Her head is flung back; thick, ink-black hair slithers down the side of her cheek. A tight, white sweater accentuates cantaloupe-like breasts and a two-handed waistline. She holds a cigarette in her hand and has a naughty look on her face.

Mom was at her best playing to an audience. Unfortunately, her theatrical career was short lived—it peaked as leading lady in a B'nai B'rith musical. After her final bow, she abandoned further career aspirations to play the supporting role in my father's growing fishing and firearms business. She settled for entertaining guests with *Sunrise, Sunset* or *My Yiddisha Momma* at family b'nai mitzvahs and weddings. Through the years, especially when she was mad, Mom would remind my father of all that she had given up. "Al, you know," she'd say, "I could have married the man I dated before I met you. He was willing to support my career."

Dad replied, "Yup. Isn't he the one who's now pumping gas at the Sunoco?"

My parents met in New York when my mother was fourteen years old. Her family had recently moved from the city to Ellenville. She found a part-time job waiting tables, where she served meatloaf and milkshakes to vacationers and locals, like my father. Mom loved telling me the story about meeting and dating my father.

"He had dark black hair, a small waist, and bulging muscles. And he also had a small nose. I wanted someone with a small nose, I didn't want big-nosed children. But I wasn't sure if I'd go on a second date with him because his pants were too short—his ankles showed. When he kept asking me out, I relented. I married him because he had a business head, and I knew that he would be successful. You should marry for those kinds of things, that's what matters. Love will come later."

In her case, it did. They were together for sixty-eight years. My father—shy, nerdy, and raised in a rural landscape—was infatuated with this sophisticated young woman from the city. He worshipped her and dedicated his life to proving to her that she had made the right choice. From the early days, when they stood shoulder-to-shoulder digging for worms to sell to fishermen for bait, to later years, when Mom insisted Dad accompany her on her mahjong cruise, they were inseparable.

When my father expanded his retail business to include manufacturing and wholesaling, Mom accompanied him to meetings around the world. Her glamour and charm wooed clients and sealed deals; she offered the perfect antidote to Dad's deadpan personality. They were a team. And they wanted me, their chubby, klutzy daughter, to lose weight, tame my hair, and acquire poise, so that I could snag my own leading man.

My mother had a hurricane-like force within her but did not possess the wherewithal to manage it. Her energy bubbled over into anxiety. She was plagued with health concerns—a headache was a brain tumor, indigestion an intestinal blockage. She distracted herself with obsessions like collecting antique watch keys, breeding tropical fish, and growing orchids. She also thrived on throwing parties, from intimate dinners to full-blown bashes, always hiring the "best" caterers, florists, musicians, and even a "candy lady" who designed chocolate party favors in the motif de jour, from edible casino chips to milk-chocolate boxes overflowing with nuts and caramels.

In later years Mom lost herself in the casinos and became a professional slot player with an ever-growing line of credit and a personal casino host who made dinner reservations for us and procured house seats for concerts by Billy Joel, Andrea Bocelli, and Elton John. Mom almost always left by intermission to get back to a hot machine.

I had tried to pry information from her about her childhood to help me understand the roots of her unrest. She'd toss me crumbs, but never revealed secrets. By interrogating my father, her best friends, and other family members, I stitched together sketches of an early life in a tenement house in upstate New York. Mom was poor; her bed was a bathtub, her mother a seamstress, and her father an electrician who fled from the family while Mom was still a teen. I would learn of darker details but not until much later.

3

Fat Girl's Camp

THE GIRL PICTURED in the magazine caught my attention. She appeared my age, ten, and she was fat—fatter than me. Her stomach protruded out from the gap between the top of her stretchy, turquoise pants and the bottom of her matching paisley top. Dimples pocked her arms and legs. Her pimpled face was swollen and she had extra chins. Her hair was disheveled, and she looked downward, away from the camera. Above her picture it read, "Before."

On the opposite side of the two-page spread, the same girl looked like she had emerged from a time machine. She was thin with a pageboy haircut and no blemishes. She wore a purple shift with a white Peter-Pan collar and cuffs. She stared directly into the camera with a full-faced smile. This caption read, "After."

I wanted to be an "After." Desperately.

I showed the advertisement to my parents. It was for a children's weight loss camp. It proclaimed, "You Too Can Lose Up to 30 Pounds this Summer."

"Can I go?"

They jumped at the opportunity.

After all, at 4'6" and 120 pounds—I was a budding spinster.

Although my parents had bribed, conned, controlled, and punished me, I still could not keep to a diet. I swapped a quarter and the orange that my mother had packed in my lunchbox for a classmate's Twinkie. I begged my grandparents for extra helpings

of macaroni and cheese. I spent my allowance on Three Muske-
teer Bars and Snickers rather than Beatles records or Margie dolls.

As my mother helped pack my duffle for camp, she said,
"These clothes will be too big for you when you come home.
We'll go out and buy you a whole new wardrobe."

On the drive to the airport my father hummed to the radio
while I tried to drown out the demons in my head. I was petrified.
I wanted to lose weight, but the reality of flying out of state by
myself to a camp where I wouldn't know anybody was too much.
It felt like I was going to throw up, and my stomach needed to
empty. It was too late to change my mind—that would devastate
my parents. I kept my fears to myself and hoped that I wouldn't
have to make Dad stop for a bathroom.

When we arrived at the airport, my father's parting words
were, "This is a once-in-a-lifetime opportunity, I hope you realize
how lucky you are. Take advantage of it. You'll have a great time.
You'll be with girls like you."

I wondered, "What was a girl like me?"

At camp we jogged to a breakfast of hardboiled eggs and
melba toast. We swam, played dodgeball, and did calisthen-
ics—anything to burn off calories. They served us veggie and
protein laden lunches and dinners. At one particularly dry fish
and soggy string bean dinner, we broke into a chorus of "We
Shall Overcome."

Once a week we gathered around the quad for the weekly
weigh-in. The bunk that lost the most weight earned a field trip.
The second week of camp, my bunk won a trip to the movies.

I don't remember what was playing—but I'll never forget
when the counselors locked hands forming a human chain in
front of the glass counter candy display. It felt like they were
saying, "Don't look. You are fat and not worthy of peanut M&Ms,
buttered popcorn, red spirally licorice, or Reese's peanut butter
cups." They gave each of us an apple.

The wide-girthed girls at camp were as clannish as the mean

girls at my school. During free time, my bunkmates gathered into cliques—no one included me. Lacking the confidence to reach out to them, I spent my free time alone.

I leafed through magazines and cut out pictures of my favorite foods: fudge cakes covered in fluffy white frosting, pancakes slathered in thick maple syrup, salty potato chips, butter pecan ice cream, and pizza, gooey with cheese. I taped those pictures around the walls of my cot. They were my friends—offering neither judgment nor disparagement.

Homesick, friendless, hungry, and miserable, I faked a severe stomachache and wound up in the hospital. The doctors could not find anything wrong but after many tests and consults, the camp directors and physicians thought it best to send me home.

After only three weeks, I had flunked fat girl's camp.

When I returned home, my mother silently unpacked my duffle. One by one, she pulled out stretch pants and smock tops, all of which would still fit just fine. There would be no shopping sprees for fashionable frocks in a smaller size.

My father said nothing. The silence now, as opposed to the one that accompanied us to the airport, was fraught with accusations of failure. I felt alone, humiliated, and worthless. I took those feelings and locked them up—like my mother did with her diamond jewelry.

That night I cried myself to sleep. I dreamt that I had superpowers. I clenched my fists, scrunched my eyes, wiggled my nose, and said, "abracadabra." And until the rising sun disrupted the delusion, I was an "after."

If I were granted those superpowers today, I'd go back in time and wrap my arms around that love-starved child. I'd kiss her forehead, both cheeks, and the top of her curly head. I'd squeeze her so tightly that she'd never again doubt her self-worth. I'd whisper into her tiny earlobe, "You are enough. You are good enough. You are loved."

It was a truth that I wouldn't fully grasp until decades later.

4

Pull the Trigger

MY PARENTS, BEFORE and after my fat camp experiment, remained relentless in their efforts to incorporate exercise into my life. One of the more ludicrous of these ideas was baton lessons. With my new silver wand in hand, I took my place in a circle of other pre-teen girls dressed in pink leotards and tights, their hair held high in ponytails or buns. *They're so skinny,* I thought, as I wrestled with my silver, shiny instrument wearing shorts and a tee shirt. I learned how to transfer the baton from one hand to the other, twirl it high into the air and sometimes, to my surprise, I caught it. I knew I'd never don one of those skimpy outfits with hanging fringe and white boots. Nor would I march down the streets of downtown Miami in the Orange Bowl parade, or any other parade for that matter. However, I had another idea.

After the third lesson, I came home and rounded up the girls in my neighborhood. "How would you like to learn how to twirl a baton?" I asked.

Five girls, ranging in age from five to ten, lined up a broom's length apart in my back yard. I collected a quarter from each of them before beginning the lesson. Only two of the girls owned batons, so I told the other three to "pretend."

Mimicking my baton teacher, I began. "Okay, class, the baton has three parts: the ball, the shaft, and the tip. Now, grab your baton in the middle and make sure your thumb is facing you." I walked up to each of the girls to check their grip. By the second class, everyone had batons. Week-by-week I continued to teach them whatever maneuver I had just learned. And I collected their quarters. By the end of the summer, I had earned almost thirty dollars. It was my first foray into business; I was good at it, I realized, and with that, I was hooked.

That fall, I looked for other opportunities to foster these early entrepreneurial desires. I honed my sales skills and sold more Girl Scout cookies than anyone else in my troop, albeit a large chunk of them to myself. I set sales records selling Christmas cards door-to-door—I'm Jewish. I babysat on weekends and earned extra money by washing dishes left in sinks and wiping crumbs from counters.

These early entrepreneurial endeavors gave me my first sense of control. I couldn't lose weight, I couldn't get my parents to soothe or comfort me, and I couldn't complete the summer at camp. But I could earn my own money.

At dinner one Friday night I said to my parents, "I'm babysitting for the Harrisons tonight. They're picking me up at seven."

Dad said, "No problem." Then he asked, "So, how much money have you made from all this babysitting?"

I did a quick calculation and said, "Almost three hundred dollars."

He finished swallowing a forkful of Mom's lasagna, and with a piece of ricotta stuck to his lower lip, said, "Never forget, money isn't everything—but it sure helps."

He smiled and gave me a slight nod, like he was proud.

It almost felt like a hug. I wanted more of this feeling—as much as I could get.

I can't recall whose idea it was, his or mine, but the next morning Dad brought me with him to work. At first, he didn't say much as we strolled side-by-side through the premises of his gun store. I took in the rows and rows of rifles standing upright in wooden floor racks and the handguns displayed in glass jewelry-like cases. A metallic, turpentine odor permeated the air. Cases of ammunition, like boxes of cookies on sale at the grocery store, were piled one on top of another in a back corner. In the opposite corner were accessories: camouflage clothing, books on hunting, and firearm cleaning supplies.

I felt overwhelmed, even a little bit scared.

Didn't guns kill people?

As if reading my mind, Dad said, "You have to handle a gun with respect. First of all, you never, ever point it at anybody." Then he took a key from his pocket and opened a glass case. He removed a revolver and pointed it toward the floor. "Now, here's how you check to see if a gun is loaded." He opened the chamber and pointed to the empty cylinders.

I nodded.

The warehouse was in a separate building and as big as my school. Forklifts made a beeping sound as they chugged down the aisles stocked with firearms, ammunition, and accessories. Dad went out of his way to introduce me to every employee, greeting them by name, and asking them about their families. From managers to gunsmiths, they'd stop whatever they were doing, stand-up, and shake Dad's hand—and sometimes mine. "You should be proud of your father," said a middle-aged, mustached accountant. The heavy-set sales manager said, "Your father is a genius in business and a kind and loyal employer." I swelled with pride, as if I was the daughter of the President.

When Dad introduced me to Juan, a warehouse foreman, he said, "Juan has worked for us for over ten years. He has three boys all under eight. Every morning Juan shows up an hour early."

"Why?" I asked, truly curious.

Juan jumped in and spoke for himself, "If something happens, like I get a flat tire, or there's a traffic jam, I don't want to be late. This way I give myself that extra cushion."

My father beamed and said, "I'll let you get back to work. I'm going to take Laura to the range and show her how to shoot."

How to shoot! I felt a titillating kind of fear, like I was about to board a roller coaster.

Dad unlocked the thick, metal door that led to a long narrow hallway with a target at the end. He said, "This is where we test guns to make sure they fire like they're supposed to." He stood in back of me, handed me a gun, and put his hands, over mine. "Now, close one eye, keep the other on the target. Hold your hands steady. When you're ready, slowly but firmly pull the trigger and aim."

Pull the trigger.

There was no way I'd let my father down now.

I took a deep breath, closed one eye, pointed at the target, and pulled. The gun made a loud bang like when they shot a man out of the cannon at the circus. "Again. Again!" Dad cheered me on. I let off a series of rounds that made my body shudder.

Dad removed the rest of the bullets from the chamber and patted my shoulder. He said, "Good job—now you know how to handle a gun and protect yourself." I thought about the firearm he kept locked in the nightstand next to his bed. A needle of fear shot up my spine. *If things get too bad, I can take that gun and end it all with one bang.*

What is wrong with me? How could I think like that?

I didn't want to die, but what if I could no longer handle living? What if I lost control for the seconds that it took to pull the trigger?

My father interrupted my rumination with, "Come on, let's get lunch."

I pried open my box of feelings and buried this latest thought at the bottom, underneath all the other fear and shame. There no one would ever discover it, I believed, and it would eventually rot with age.

I wanted more—not of the shooting or the scary thoughts, but of the business. From that day on, I went to work with my father at his store every Saturday and during summer vacations.

I learned how to ring the cash register. When a customer handed me a bill, I left it on the shelf. "In this way," my father explained, "if someone gives you a ten, they can't later claim that it was a twenty." He showed me how to check for counterfeit bills by holding them up to the light. Whenever someone purchased a handgun, I had to fill out forms asking their name, address, and the purpose of their purchase. I thought that was stupid—nobody was ever going to say, "I bought it to rob a bank." I was also supposed to watch for shoplifters, but I missed it when a man put a rifle down each of his pant legs and walked stiffly out the door.

What stuck with me most about this experience was the importance of merchandizing. To illustrate this point, Dad put a basket of batteries by the cash register with a sign that read, "33 cents each or 3 for a dollar." Whenever a customer said, "I'll take three," Dad nudged me in the side with a conspiring nod. He said, P.T. Barnum was right, "There's a sucker born every minute."

My paternal grandfather isolated himself in the back office of the warehouse. Whenever I peeked in to visit, I'd find him hunched over inventory and sales reports. He was always happy to see me.

"Laurichika!" he'd say, as he opened a folding chair and placed it next to his worn-out vinyl desk chair. "Sit down. Sit down." He'd pat the seat. "How's your day going?" Grandpa was a short, balding, religious man who wore tightly belted trousers pulled up high upon his waist. According to family lore, he created one of the first self-service grocery stores in upstate New York. In the "old days" customers had to ask the grocer to fetch their bread, milk, and eggs. Grandpa came up with the idea of aisles. In this way shoppers could take their own cart and peruse the shelves. Walking by jars of applesauce, boxes of cereal, and cans of soup, they were likely to buy more than they had put on their shopping list.

Grandpa loved giving me math problems. "What is twelve times two plus thirty?" he'd ask.

I had to come up with the answer in my head. Thinking for a minute, I'd say, "Fifty-four"

"Great. You have a good kepeleh (head). Honey, remember there are not always adding machines around when you make business deals. You need to be quick, ahead of the next guy. You need to know how to figure out a fifteen percent tip or the cost of a dress that's on sale for thirty percent off." He was right—decades latter these skills gave me a one-up in negotiations and business deals.

Working at the gun store, selling cookies and greeting cards, and giving those baton lessons—all of it took me out of myself. I thought more about doing a good job and less about how I looked while doing that job. I earned my own money. I understood from watching my father that money meant power.

When I looked at my body in the mirror, I still felt the old shame—but if I only looked into my eyes, I saw hope. Perhaps my future would offer more than my past.

5

Creating a Trail

THE OPPORTUNITY TO begin creating that future surfaced during my senior year of high school. My homeroom teacher, Miss Allen, her gray hair pinned into a bun and wearing what Mom would have called a muumuu, said, "I know you're all excited and perhaps nervous about graduating and going to college or getting a job. Let's go around the room and share your plans for after high school."

A mixed palette of pride, angst, and resignation spilled out as we shared our post-graduation futures. "Florida State University," said the greasy-haired girl on my right. Twirling blond curls around her finger, the girl next to her said, "The University of South Florida." The boy in the next seat, who looked like he was trying to grow a mustache, said, "Dade County Community College."

With each student's declaration, a heaviness mounted in my chest. I, too, had planned on staying in state. Living in Miami, at the southeast tip of the peninsula, colleges in Gainesville or Tallahassee had seemed adventurous enough. But now I wondered if this was my chance to escape from a culture that valued flat stomachs, materialism, and ostentation to one that honored intellectual curiosity and introspection.

It had been an eye-opening year. In English we studied Henry David Thoreau and Ralph Waldo Emerson, transcendentalists from the mid-1800s. I was enamored with the ideals of simplification, connection to nature, and alignment with the universe. I scotch-taped quotes onto the cover of my denim-blue, three-ring notebook. One of my favorites was Emerson's, "Do not go where the path may lead, go instead where there is no path and leave a trail." I had no idea what my trail would look like—but I was intrigued with the idea that I could create one.

Years later, in a gift store in Atlantic City, I found a parchment-colored plaque with those words engraved in large black letters. It still sits on a shelf in my home office.

Energized with the idea of leaving Miami, on the way home from school that day, I stopped at a bookstore and bought a thick college reference book. At home in my bed, I propped a pillow behind my head and leaned the manual against my bent knees. I leafed through the descriptions of East Coast schools, circling those with strong academic credentials that offered majors in psychology. I figured that by getting out of Florida and into cooler weather, I could avoid bikini-laden coeds sunbathing on campus. I also hoped that a strong academic environment would attract students seeking intellectual pursuits rather than smaller waistlines.

By the following morning, I had narrowed my search to two options: Clark University in Worcester, Massachusetts, known for their top-rate psychology department and Emory University in Atlanta, which also had strong social sciences and was a twelve-hour drive from home.

I would be the first in my family to attend college. My parents graduated from high school but, as my father said, "we didn't have the luxury of further education, we had to get right to work." My brother, Jay, three years younger than I, took his time jumping into academics. With his jet-black hair and big blue eyes, he had better things, like girls, to focus on. However, my father wouldn't let him veer far off course. We still laugh remembering a dinner when Dad, with his glasses falling low on his nose, looked over Jay's report card, and said, "You are so lazy. You'll probably end up marrying a woman who is already pregnant. The only positive thing I can say about this report card is at least you don't cheat."

Dad was wrong. Not only did Jay go to college but he went on to get a master's in business. Ironically, he followed in Dad's footsteps, and built a successful business.

My sister, Gail, the baby of the family and eight years younger than I am, was in many ways the daughter my parents truly desired. With her ink black hair, petite frame, wide eyes, and a full-faced smile she looked just like my mother. She also earned a master's degree in business and followed a successful career path.

My parents were supportive, albeit passive participants in my college search. They schlepped with me to tour both schools. First, we flew to Boston and drove to Worcester to visit Clark. On the way there, I asked if we could stop in Concord so that I could see Walden Pond, where Thoreau spent two years living in a cabin in the woods. Perhaps if I walked in the philosopher's footsteps, his wisdom and insights might rub off on me.

It wasn't far out of our way. Dad pulled into a parking lot that bordered the site. We all looked out the window but a thick sheet of ice covered the blue waters of the pond. Mom said, "Did you see enough?"

"No, I want to go out."

"Then we'll wait for you in the car, it's freezing out there." Dad chimed in.

I zipped up my fleece-lined coat, put on a hat, and gloves. Wearing new boots with traction, I trekked through the snow to the border of the lake, taken in by the barren stillness. I imagined Thoreau living here for two years and contemplated what it might have been like for him. Lost in my fantasies, I felt a presence, a sacredness, like I did at synagogue when the rabbi opened the arc. And in that silence, Thoreau's words came to me, "It's not what you look at that matters, it's what you see."

It's not what I look at but what I see.

There was that hope again—a shift, a way out. I could stop *looking* at all the superficial things and start *seeing* that which really mattered.

A skill that would take a lifetime to master.

Back in the car, Dad said, "Was it worth standing out there in the cold?"

Mom, said, "Al, let's go, I want to check into the hotel."

I smiled. "Thank you. Yes, it was worth it."

THE GROUNDS OF Emory's original campus in Oxford, Georgia consisted of freestanding buildings that encircled a large grassy area, the quad. Students gathered in groups; they looked like hippies. Some of the women were braless, peace signs dangled from their necks, and their jeans had holes in the knees and thighs. A bearded professor walked by and waved. When one of the women waved back, I noticed her hairy underarm.

After touring the campus, I was invited to observe a psychology class. Sitting in the back of the room I was riveted as the professor explained Maslow's theory of self-actualization. "There is a hierarchy of needs: physiological, safety, belonging, esteem, and finally, for only a few, where we reach our full potential—self-actualization." Actualization. I leaned forward and wished I had brought a yellow-lined legal pad with me to take notes. A way to reach a state of bliss, and weight or wealth weren't even mentioned.

I was sold on Emory and would spend my first two years in the Mayberry-like town of Oxford before transferring to the main campus in Atlanta. I also liked Clark, but after my summer camp fiasco, I thought it better to stay within driving distance of home.

Oxford had a population of under 2,000, and there was only one traffic light in the town. My father, with his indomitable humor said, "I wonder if I can make a right turn on red?" A few months later, I ran into Charlie, the policeman who patrolled the campus. I asked him about the right on red. He stroked his chin, slicked back his hair, and then closed his eyes as if trying to recall a specific regulation. Finally, he said, "I'm not sure. What are other cities doing?"

The first week of classes I met Meredith, a tall, lanky girl from a small town in the South. She had taped a sign above her bed that read, "God never gives us more than we can handle." I envied her. I would have loved to believe that a higher power would take care of me. Whenever life seemed too hard, I could simply trust that it would be okay. And how I wished that I believed I would never have more than I could manage.

A few days into the semester, I stopped by her room to see if she wanted to go with me to the bookstore. Poised at her door, I overheard her talking on the phone with her mother. She said, "You won't believe it, I found out that a girl down the hall is a Jew. I'm staying away."

It was my first taste of anti-Semitism. Grandpa, in-between math quizzes, had told me that there were people who would hate me just because I was Jewish. And in Sunday School I had learned about the Holocaust and other atrocities against the Jews. But I had thought that was the past.

How naïve. I tucked away the remark but never forgot it.

I made many other friends at school, Jewish and non-Jewish. I took courses on psychology, sociology, and philosophy and spent much of my time sitting cross-legged on the grounds of the quad discussing Aristotle, Freud, and Erik Erickson with like-minded seekers.

Thanks to diet pills—actually speed—prescribed by my pediatrician the summer before college, I had lost some weight and gained some confidence. I let my hair grow long, and I could fit into regular-sized, bell-bottom jeans, at least for the time being. I was attracted to the long-haired, bearded boys thirsty for introspection, discourse, sex, and drugs.

I think back to the night that a handful of us gathered together in our friend Joe's dorm room. John Lennon and Yoko Ono sang in the background pleading for peace. I sank into a bean bag chair, passed a joint, and argued for free will over determinism.

"We choose how we want to live our lives," I insisted in a voice loud enough to be heard over the music.

The scent of incense, which we had lit in a failed attempt to overpower the marijuana, permeated the air as Joe ran his fingers through his long beard and countered, "That's easy for you to say, but what about those born in circumstances that dictate their choices?"

I was angry. I needed to believe that I had control over my trajectory. "Do you really believe life is pre-ordained? If so, what is the point?" I asked.

We never reached consensus, but during those late-night debates, I felt a sense of belonging. I had found other people who enjoyed dissecting ideas rather than outfits. They were interested in understanding rather than judging, and in their presence, I was valued.

During the semester breaks I worked hard. I spent my first summer as a camp coordinator, overseeing counselors and juggling activity schedules. The second summer, I prepared basic tax returns. My final summer, I took classes enabling me to graduate in three years rather than the usual four.

In that last year, I moved to an apartment in Atlanta. A long-haired boy from Baltimore came to visit my roommate's boyfriend. He fell in love with me—and I fell in love with being loved. He was a kind, gentle man who accepted me without judgment. When I was awarded a stipend to attend a graduate psychology program in Baltimore, he gave me the confidence and motivation to make the move.

We were living together for a few months when, unwittingly, he answered an early morning phone call from my mother.

"Good morning," he said, stifling a yawn.

My mother, not willing to partake in niceties, said, "Put my daughter on the phone."

He said, "She's in the shower."

"I'll wait." she said.

Wrapped in a towel, I picked up the receiver, and my father was on the extension. They said, "What are you doing with a man in your house at 8 a.m.? What is going on?"

"Don't worry, it's no big deal," I said and looked to my boyfriend for confirmation.

Not long afterwards, he proposed.

He loved me and he was Jewish, that seemed enough. My parents flew to Baltimore to meet his parents. Both sides were exuberant. My parents' biggest fear, that I'd be a spinster, was assuaged; his parents were delighted because their son was marrying a "go-getter" from a "nice family."

Friends and relatives threw me a shower with crustless sandwiches and Jell-O molds. I felt ridiculous, like a fraud, as I sat in a cushioned armchair under a white umbrella. I went through all the motions: I registered for china, crystal, and sterling. I kept my nails manicured to emphasize a one-carat, marquee diamond ring. And I went with my parents to "the" bridal shop in DC where I picked out a white, lacy, slenderizing gown. The wedding would take place, under my mother's supervision, at their country club in Miami.

The bridal party, wearing pink gowns and black tuxedos, gathered together in the vestibule. When the flutist pursed her lips to begin the processional, I panicked; my palms were sweaty, my forehead felt hot. The wedding planner commanded, "Look from left to right. Smile at your guests. Walk slowly, purposefully. This is your moment." Then he placed a gloved hand on my back and nudged me down the rose-lined aisle.

I made my way through a haze of doubt. The whiff from the orchids, spirituality of the Chuppah, and clear notes from the strings of the harp conspired to mock my uncertainty. I looped my arm into my father's, proceeded as planned, and wondered, as I still did often, "Do I look fat?"

PART II

CLIMBING UP

6

3,000 Pocketbooks

"MAKE A WISH. You have to make a wish."

Friends crowded around the combination dining/living room of our townhouse to celebrate my 24th birthday. As I bent over to blow out the candles on my cake, I didn't need to think hard. Since the wedding, I had gained back all the pounds, plus more, that I had lost from my amphetamine-induced pre-college diet. I had said to my husband, "I guess I never lost them—just misplaced them for a while." He had enough sense not to comment.

I closed my eyes, looked to the sky, and wished for one day to live as a sexy woman, like the models in *Cosmopolitan* or like Elly May from the television show, *Beverly Hillbillies*.

For those twenty-four hours I would walk with my head held high, my long blond hair swaying in rhythm with the wind. I'd walk with a jiggle, but just the right kind of jiggle. Men would follow in my confident wake, mesmerized by my tush. They'd take me to fancy restaurants for dinner, and I'd pat my flat stomach and say, "No desserts for me."

My date would answer, "What do you have to worry about? Your body is perfect. How about the double fudge cake or an ice cream sundae?"

I'd go clothes shopping looking at the size fours, perhaps a size six in a top to accommodate my perfect braless bosoms. I'd swirl in front of the three-way mirror and try to appear humble when the other customers said, awe in their voices, "You look amazing."

I'd try on bathing suits—the ones that revealed the most skin, not the ones that promised to "hide ten pounds."

I'd go to the local coffee shop and wink at the men who insisted, "You go first." When they paid for my cappuccino, I'd offer a sly smile and a slight nod to show my gratitude.

I'd pretend not to notice when they fought over who opened my door or picked up a lipstick that I just happened to drop to the ground. I'd wear high heels, even when I went to the grocery store.

I'd act a teensy bit snobby and remote instead of genuine and caring, just to see how it felt. And I'd shout, "Whoo-hoo" when a cute boy made a touchdown. I'd sit on laps when hanging out with friends and on shoulders for wrestling in the pool.

The restlessness of the partygoers shook me from my reverie.

"So, what did you wish for?" someone asked.

"You know it's bad luck to reveal birthday wishes. And please, I'd like a sliver of my cake."

THE NEXT DAY, back to work as a salesclerk in a woman's clothing store, I tucked the wish into that locked box of things I didn't want to think about and concentrated on my job. This was my chance to put into action the sales and marketing skills I had learned from my father. One morning, a few weeks after I started, I came to work and found the manager and other employees straightening racks, redressing mannequins, and polishing mirrors.

"What's going on?" I asked.

"A vice president of our company is coming in from New York tomorrow," our manager explained. "He's on a tour of the top revenue branches and ours is on the list. We have to make sure everything is perfect and impress him."

The next day, a well-dressed man in an expensive-looking suit and tie walked in followed by an entourage of corporate bigwigs. Our manager and assistant manager greeted him, and they began a wall-to-wall survey of the store. When they passed by me, I said, "Excuse me. If you have a few minutes before you leave, I have some ideas I'd like to share with you."

My manager gave me a look that said, "I should fire you now." Another lesson learned: tread carefully before going above or around your boss.

The vice president said, "Of course."

At the end of the day, he asked me to step outside of the store and into the mall. Pointing to a bench in front of the food court, he said, "Please, sit down."

Gathering my courage, I took in the aroma of hot pretzels dunked in butter and salt and the screeches of children straddling miniature plastic ponies on the three-person merry-go-round. Then I focused my attention on the big boss.

He was a tall, balding, fifty-something man wearing a well-cut, obviously expensive suit and shiny leather shoes. He set his briefcase down between us as I pulled out a sheet of yellow-lined paper from my purse and gave him my suggestions to increase sales one-by-one.

"Number One, I've noticed that people tend to buy the exact outfit we put on the mannequins. They want the top, pants, and even the belt and scarf. So why don't we dress more mannequins and highlight more displays?"

He nodded in agreement.

"Number Two, our employees greet customers by saying, 'Can I help you?' This gets a yes or usually no response. Why don't we train them to ask leading questions like, 'Can you believe they're forecasting snow? I'd love to show you the new coats that just came in.'"

Now he pulled out his own pad and pencil from his briefcase and said, "Please continue."

When I was finished with my list, he thanked me and asked, "Anything else?"

"That's all for now."

Looking back, I suppose that because I saw my father as the penultimate boss, I had no fear of speaking my mind to others in authority. Dad had instilled in me the importance of maximizing revenue, and that was what I wanted to convey to this executive.

We walked back into the store together. I put my purse into the back room and then helped a customer who was looking for an outfit to wear on a blind date.

I hoped I wouldn't get fired.

The next morning, my manager said, "The company would like you to manage our store on Maryland's Eastern Shore. There are no manager openings here."

I was not going to relocate but accepted a promotion to assistant manager.

I wondered whether management noticed that I couldn't fit into their clothing. They carried sizes four to fourteen, and I was an eighteen.

About six months into my new role, I was working the late shift when I approached a balding, mustached man who was perusing the racks without purpose.

"It looks like you're a little lost. Let me help you," I offered.

"It's my wife's birthday tomorrow," he said.

"Do you know what size she wears?" I asked.

"No." He looked around at other customers and pointed to a woman who was going through the sale rack.

"She's about her size."

I approached the woman, "Please forgive this intrusion, but that gentleman is trying to surprise his wife for her birthday and thinks she wears your size."

The customer played along, "I wear an eight."

Within the hour, I sold him a thousand dollars' worth of tops, pants, and dresses. As I was ringing up the sale, he asked, "I have a friend who owns a women's clothing store in this mall. He needs a manager. Can he call you?"

Why not? I figured.

The next day his friend called and asked me to meet him at his store after work.

During my lunch break, I walked around the mall to survey his store. It was a mess. Tops hung willy-nilly from hangers— without coordinating pants or skirts. The display windows were uninviting, without a color scheme or fashion pull. The walls were dark, the lights dim. I thought, *with free reign I could turn this store around.*

When I met with the owner that night he said, "My friend was impressed with your sales skills. He told me it was the most money he'd ever spent on clothing for his wife, and she loved everything. I want you to manage this store. You can hire whoever you want, I'll give you complete freedom. I'll pay you twenty percent more than your current salary and give you a percentage of increase in the store's revenue."

He showed me the books. I calculated the difference in volume between this store and the one I managed. Without much effort, I could triple the sales. I took the job.

The first step was to motivate the employees. As I had learned from watching my father, I made it a point to inquire about their families and stay current with the ups and downs of their lives. Those who worked hard were given raises, while others were let go. I instituted weekly sales contests and hired Bonnie, a free-spirited, highly talented window designer, who transformed the former mess of a store into a high-end boutique. I connected with the customers and knew the regulars by name. And like I had proffered to that executive on the bench at the mall, I instructed Bonnie to parade full outfits on mannequins, t-stands, and other displays.

A year later I was driving a company car and making more money than my old manager. At the time I was unaware of the metaphorical ladder. Now, looking back, I see that I had begun the ascent.

AFTER DINNER ONE night, as my husband and I sat on the sofa watching a rerun of *MASH*, my new boss telephoned me. I was taken aback because he had never before called me at home.

He sounded anxious, his voice quivering as he said, "We have a problem. Our buyer quit. He was scheduled to go to New York next week for the spring buying season. I want you to go."

Me, a buyer? I had no idea how to begin. But I was eager, albeit nervous, for the opportunity.

I spent the following week evaluating the merchandise at competing boutiques and department stores, looking for brands that I thought would sell in our stores. The clientele was made up of women in their late teens to mid-forties—and those who wanted to dress as if they were a part of that age group. I checked out tops, pants, jumpsuits, and leather coats and made lists of manufacturers that appealed to me and that I thought would sell. I looked up their New York addresses and made appointments with reps. Clutching my new brown leather briefcase which contained a budget and my scouting notes, I got off the train at Penn Station and made my way to the center of the garment district, wearing my most slenderizing plus-sized black business suit and comfortable walking shoes.

I was initially overwhelmed by the crowds and the chaos. I squeezed into elevators packed tight with other buyers and prayed that the antiquated lifts would reach the high floors. I walked through long, dark hallways into brightly-lit showrooms jammed full of merchandise. Sales representatives, with the dexterity of a magician, pulled garments from racks, each one the next season's "best seller."

I took notes and calculated costs. I imagined myself as the size six of my birthday fantasy—what would I buy? Tapping into intuition and relying on instinct, I placed the orders. My do-it-yourself course in buying was a success. The clothes sold and revenues skyrocketed. My biggest coup, however, was due to my father. He was on a business trip in South America when he called me breathless with excitement and said, "I have a chance to buy 3,000 genuine leather pocketbooks for a dollar each. You have to let me know immediately. "

There wasn't time to check with the store owner; I had to take a chance. I got that rollercoaster feeling again, closed my eyes, inhaled, and said, "Do it."

When the purses arrived, we arranged one hundred of them on a table in the front of the store with a big square sign in red letters that read, "SALE $99.00." Each morning we refilled the table until the best bags were gone. Then we lowered the price to $79.00. The last fifty pocketbooks sold for $29.

I was promoted to vice president and put in charge of the five-store chain.

It didn't take me long to learn that the best way to capture a customer's attention and make a sale was when she was the most vulnerable: stripped down to her bra and underwear in the dressing room. She'd slide the curtain to one side leaving me enough space to hand her a flattering dress to cover cellulite-pocked thighs or pants made from spandex-type fabrics to camouflage her stomach.

"How's it going?" I'd ask through the fabric barrier.

"I'm not sure. I think it makes me look fat," she'd say.

"Come out and let's look in the three-way mirror," I'd coax.

I was flabbergasted. There was seldom any correlation between a woman's perception of her appearance and reality.

"This makes my rear look too big," an impish young girl exclaimed.

A leggy, curvy blonde turned her head over her shoulder to scrutinize her behind and said, "I hate my hips."

I'd have traded her hips for my own and thrown in my car to seal the deal.

If women like her hated their appearances, what was wrong with the system?

I had not yet found a customer who was proud of her body— rather, most of them inflated their flaws and, in doing so, diminished their self-worth. For the first time, I began to question the rules of a game in which no one ever won. Why did we blindly adhere to a set of standards that left us feeling inadequate?

But I knew from painful experience that it was not easy to reject society's pervasive messages about the importance of appearance. It seemed that every time I took a few steps forward in changing my perspective and focusing on confidence-boosting career moves, old insecurities set me back a wrung—and none more than the knock-out punch from my mother when planning my sister's wedding.

Despite our age difference, Gail and I were always close. When she called me from Boston to tell me about Harry, I was elated.

"Laura, there's this guy in my finance class. He's so smart and hot."

"Tell me more," I said.

"He's a little over six-feet tall with dark black hair and piercing eyes. He's quick and funny. He's from the area and.... there's just something about him. I think he's the one."

Not long after that call, they were engaged. Harry was as handsome as Gail was beautiful; they looked like the couple on top of the wedding cake. My parents could not have been happier. It was my mother's final opportunity to host a society-page worthy affair.

Later, when rehashing the wedding, my father said, "I gave Mom an unlimited budget, and she exceeded it." My mother said, "Oh, Al!"

Mom hired a designer for custom-made bridesmaids' dresses. I flew to Miami to meet with him. He was slight with brown, shoulder-length hair and wore earrings and pointy white shoes. I was instantly self-conscious in the face of his fashion-forward style and coolness.

My mother introduced us, turned to the designer, and said, "This is Laura, the one I told you about. Is there anything you can do with her so that she doesn't detract from the beauty of the wedding?"

I lost thirty pounds for the wedding. I gained them all back before my sister returned home from her honeymoon.

7

Sending the Nanny on Field Trips

AFTER THREE YEARS of marriage, I was the heaviest I'd ever been in my life. My old coping mechanism, drowning out feelings with food, was in full swing. By chomping on fried chicken wings, I could subdue a gnawing sense of dissatisfaction.

I should have delved into these feelings—but instead I chided myself. "You should be so grateful. You have a good husband, a great job, live in a nice neighborhood. What is your problem?" Duly chastised, I submerged myself in my work and talked with my husband about starting a family. He was on board. It seemed like all of our friends and the other couples in our suburban community were pregnant, talking about getting pregnant, or wheeling strollers down the sidewalk that led to the community pool.

When my obstetrician confirmed, "You're pregnant," I tossed those feelings of discontent to the side and fell in love with my growing fetus. I was—we were—ecstatic. I bought a copy of *What to Expect When You're Expecting*, and we meandered through furniture stores and ordered the crib, bureau, and changing table. I spotted a white, wicker rocking chair that I had to buy because it invoked a vision of me holding my newborn in my arms while singing, "Hush little baby don't say a word."

And I also researched childcare options.

A neighbor had invited me for coffee to celebrate my pregnancy. She had three boys and seemed always harried. On our way to the kitchen, she stopped and said, "Look how we redid the family room."

I took in the three desks, each with a child's name hanging above it, the toybox spilling over with wooden blocks, tinker toys, and rubber superheroes, and the model train tracks that circled the floor. She said, "Go help yourself, I'll be right there. I need to throw the wash into the dryer."

We never had that coffee. Her boys ran into the house screaming. One of them had fallen from the backyard swing. He was fine but needed comforting.

Was this where I was heading?

I wanted more. And yet, dare I ask for more?

It made me feel like a bad mother to admit that even had we not needed the earnings from my job, I would have chosen to return to the office and pursue my career. I craved the ego-fulfillment and challenges of the workplace. By increasing revenues, selecting fashion trends, and helping women feel good about themselves by finding the right outfits, I was somebody. I was challenged, excited, and in my element. I did not want to spend my days changing diapers and emptying dishwashers.

But here came that insidious feeling, the curse of the working mother: guilt.

I wasn't like my neighbor. I simply wasn't content to stay home. I wanted to make my own mark, figure out my purpose, and, like I learned from that college professor, reach for actualization. I was too embarrassed to share these feelings with anyone, even my husband, so I wrote to my unborn child,

There is so much I want for you, yet I must tread lightly not to fulfill myself through you but to provide you with the confidence to fulfill your own potential. Your life has given birth to new ideals in mine. How I hope you can feel the love I have for you. I want you to feel free to be yourself in the fullest sense—to love and be loved without false weights or boundaries. Do not wait for others to grant you what you need, go after it yourself. Do not be afraid to express your emotions and frailties. Appreciate the beauty in life.

My beautiful baby, please forgive me when I'm overprotective or seem unfair, for I know I won't always tell you, but it will be out of love. Also, forgive me if it seems that I'm not devoting my whole life to you. One can only love one's child, like her spouse, as much as she loves herself. I will work to learn to love myself and reach my own potential while loving you. And I thank God that he has blessed me and seen me fit to carry you.

I gave birth to an almost nine-pound boy, Danny. Three years later came his brother, Andy, and seven years after that, my daughter, Jackie. As I had predicted, in spite of my love for my babies, I was chomping to get back to work after each delivery. All of their births were C-sections, and I was back to my job within weeks. Childcare was always challenging. We ran through the gamut of alternatives from daycare to live-in nannies.

And, as I had suspected, I was better at reading profit and loss statements than reading Dr. Seuss, happier at building teams than Lego houses. Even though I spent more time on business trips than field trips, I'd like to think that I was there when it mattered most, however. I cheered for my children's goals at soccer games and consoled them when baseball pitches went askew. I washed cotton-candy fingers at Disney on Ice and stayed through the finale, even though I was bored. I sat in tiny chairs at parent-teacher conferences and never missed a visiting day at camp. With the help of nannies and daycare, I learned to do it all, just not perfectly. I tolerated unmade beds and dirty dishes. My children tolerated store-brought brownies and drugstore Halloween costumes.

We had moved from the townhouse into a two-story detached house, set back on a court with a yard and a neighborhood full of kids. The other moms would gather in bunches at the bus stop, waiting for their kids to come home, while I was still at work. They threw potluck lunches during snowstorms; I was too busy inspecting sales reports to attend. And they vied for coveted seats on the school bus for field trips while I sent my nanny.

One Saturday morning, I was outside getting the paper when one of my neighbors came over and introduced herself.

She said, "It seems like you and I are the only working mothers in this development. I'd like to get to know you—it gets lonely. How about going for a walk this afternoon?"

We are still friends—shared feelings dilute guilt. We regret, however, that we hadn't been kinder and gentler with our younger selves.

AT THIRTY-ONE YEARS old, when my boys were seven and four, I bought a new pair of jeans, a stack of yellow-lined legal pads, a slew of file folders, and walked through the doors of the University of Maryland School of Law as a part-time student.

I had left the women's clothing store chain to help my husband in his children's clothing stores. For a while, I enjoyed enticing pig-tailed little girls to try on princess-like dresses and helping overwhelmed mothers find onesies with snaps, but before long I was antsy for more. I realized, however, that the legalities of the business intrigued me: how to negotiate leases, terminate contracts, and fire an employee without legal repercussions.

After the first semester, I enrolled full time so that I could graduate with my class in three years. Energized by the subtleties of property, torts, and constitutional law, I immersed myself into my studies in the same way I devoured a loaf of bread and a jar of peanut butter.

Perhaps my eagerness was a bit much. Like the time I raised my hand in a legal procedure class and said, "I'm sorry, but I have one more question. I promise this will be the last one."

The professor said, "Now Mrs. Black, do you think anyone here believes that?"

And then in the winter of my last year, I learned that I was pregnant. As I've told my daughter, Jackie, as soon as she was old enough to understand, "You were not a mistake, you were a gift." Although (and I left this part out) at the time it felt like a crisis.

I could no longer ignore a persistent nagging feeling that my marriage wasn't working. I knew, on some level, that I had made a mistake. Yet, he was a good father, a good man, and I had made a commitment. I was willing to stick it out. However, like a car with deflated tires, it was tough to stay on course. The financial and emotional weight of a third child could flatten all hopes of repair.

My obstetrician advised, "You are over thirty, so we need to do some tests. You already have two boys. Let's make sure this is a healthy fetus and determine the sex. Wait until you get the results, it might help you decide."

I left his office and broke down crying. Resting my head on the steering wheel, trying to gain control, I knew the answer. I already loved this baby. Whatever the sex, it was mine and I was keeping it.

Concentrating on my law school studies, I graduated near the top of my class. I was an editor for the prestigious Law Review and a member of the moot court board. On a clear, azure day in May, I walked across the stage, shook hands with the dean, and accepted my diploma. My husband sat between the boys and next to my parents. They all cheered me on when I received honors.

The black graduation gown covered my angst but not my pregnant belly.

Jackie was born in early June—on the same day (ten years later) as her eldest brother. Sitting up in my hospital bed, post-C-section, I looked to my bedside table, piled high with bar prep books—contracts, torts, real property. They made me nauseous. The bar exam was in July, and I was running out of time. My ambivalence about having another child in a strained marriage filled me with guilt-induced angst.

I saw a therapist.

He said, "Skip the July bar and take it later. This is too much stress. Bond with your daughter and help her big brothers adjust."

He gave me what I craved: permission.

The night before the exam my husband said, "What are you doing tomorrow?"

"Nothing."

"Why don't you take the exam. You graduated near the top of your class; you know your stuff. What's the worst that can happen? Here are some sharpened pencils."

This moment made all the difference in the world, and I will be forever grateful for his support.

That night I dreamt that the bar exam was a ruse. There was a secret society of lawyers. Once you showed up, they gave you a special pin and you were part of the club.

The next morning, I put those pencils in my purse along with some high-energy granola bars and a small bag of nuts and drove to the testing site. As my friends and I waited for the doors to open, I told them about my dream. The fantasy spread through the anxious students faster than news of a classmate's illicit affair.

The doors opened and we were instructed to take our seats. Then we were bombarded with a litany of dos and don'ts. I can't remember the precise instructions, but I do recall the urge to vomit. I picked up a sharpened #2 pencil and began reading questions and coloring in ovals.

8

Black Suits and Extra-Wide Flats

I HUNG MY diplomas on the walls of my colorless office, located near the end of the hall in a tall office building that housed an upper-crust law firm. Then I positioned pictures of my children around the perimeter of my desk: three-month-old Jackie in a boldly patterned onesie; Andy, then seven years old, dressed in his soccer uniform and kicking a ball; and Danny, at ten, poised for power in a long-sleeve dress shirt and pants. And I placed the plaque of that Emerson quote, some figurines of women lawyers, and a replica of the scales of justice on the top shelf of my bookcase. After adjusting the height of my high-back, black vinyl desk chair, I got to work.

I had passed the bar exam. Now, with the help of senior associates and junior partners, I learned how to draft motions (like those for summary judgment) arguing that "there was no genuine dispute as to material facts and the case must be dismissed as a matter of law." I took depositions of witnesses and experts to set the groundwork for upcoming cases, and I spent untold hours researching points of law and establishing precedent.

I lasted two years.

On a sticky Friday afternoon, as I rounded the corner to the elevator, one of the partners stopped me and said, "We need to prep for a case we thought would settle but didn't. We'll go to trial next week. This weekend we need you to work on some motions, etc."

Andy was in soccer playoff games that weekend. I had promised him that I'd be there. I wanted to be there. I decided in that moment that no matter what, I was going to be there.

This was not the lifestyle that I wanted. I was willing to put in the hours and effort, but around my schedule. I respected the firm and enjoyed the intellectual stimulation, but I did not want to spend my time defending other people's businesses.

Over dinner that night, my husband shook his head in exasperation and said, "What? Really? You want to quit?"

Danny and Andy stopped eating their spaghetti and looked at me in disbelief.

I tried to explain, "Let's say someone sues my client for negligence. I can try to get the case dismissed or eventually prove they aren't liable. If I'm successful, after a lot of time, energy, and legal fees, except in rare situations, my client is back where they started before the lawsuit."

"But isn't that your job?" asked Danny.

"Yes. And I feel good when we win. But I'd rather expend that energy where there is more monetary upside for us."

In spite of my family's frustration, I gave the appropriate notice and felt like a failure. *What would I do now?* A different law firm was not the answer. I was with one of the best; it was the practice I was leaving, not the people. I had put my family through the stress of law school and the bar examination. I had finally found a way to make my parents proud—their daughter, the lawyer. I too felt pride in what I had accomplished.

I circled through other options but came up empty. Friends and family warned me, "You need to rethink this decision. You're making the biggest mistake of your life." I paid my penance in self-torture. Then, like the sun breaking through a sky of dark clouds, an idea began to take shape.

I had spent much of the two years at the law firm taking depositions, gathering information from witnesses and parties as part of the discovery process of a case. What if I could leverage this experience? Before I had time to talk myself out of it, I called an attorney that had left my firm to start his own practice. I said, "Do you need someone to help with your overflow litigation needs? I could take depositions for you."

He was familiar with my work and hopped on the idea. "I can keep you busy for about twenty hours a week. What do you charge?"

I had no idea.

I thought about my grandfather and how he insisted that I learn to calculate numbers in my head. I did some quick multiplication and addition to determine what I needed to charge to match my law firm salary.

Projecting more confidence than I felt, I gave him my newly determined hourly rate.

"When can you start?" he said.

Thank-you, Grandpa. I envisioned that wise, balding man, with a twinkle in his eyes saying, "Laurichka, you did good."

That night I slept soundly for the first time since I had quit my job.

I also placed an advertisement in the local legal newspaper proposing to help other attorneys with their overflow work, offering to write briefs and motions and to research legal issues. Within a few weeks I had a handful of clients and a business was blooming.

Not long into this venture, Mark, a friend from law school called me.

"I heard through the grapevine what you've started," he said. "I think it's a great idea. Maybe we can do it together. Let's meet for coffee."

We made a date for the following week. I hung up the phone and it rang again.

"Can we meet now?" he asked.

"Yes." It was the best business decision I ever made.

The idea was for us to divide the assignments. I'd take on the litigation work and Mark would concentrate on real estate and tax. Despite our plan, I had misgivings. One morning, as I reluctantly prepared for an afternoon deposition, I was frustrated. I had no interest in questioning the potential witness. I did not want to practice law. I wanted to build a business. We needed to tweak our plan.

The next day, Mark and I talked.

We agreed that we had developed a promising model. The assignments were flowing in and there was a clear need for our services.

We were also keenly aware that we had only practiced law for a couple of years. What if instead of sending ourselves out, we put together a pool of attorneys with a wide array of specializations and sent *them* out? We could recruit and manage these temporary lawyers rather than doing the actual work ourselves.

Mark did the necessary research to check the viability of this new staffing model. He found inexpensive office space and we furnished it on a shoestring: old chairs from my basement, a desk from his. Without money to hire staff, we answered the phones as well as interviewed and checked the references of applicants for our pool. There were plenty of attorneys looking for contract work. Between those that had fled the profession because of work-life balance, seasoned lawyers looking to steer into other jobs or industries while earning a living, and recent law school graduates, we put together an impressive cadre of professionals. Later, we added paralegals, legal secretaries, and other support staff.

Dressed in a black suit and extra-wide flats, I met with the managing partners of law firms and Corporate 500 CEOs and convinced them of the benefits of supplementing their workforce with temporary staffing. They were intrigued as they calculated the potential cost-savings of transferring from a fixed to a variable staffing model.

During this time, in the early 1990s, women were finally making significant inroads into high-level positions in law firms and corporations, upending old stereotypes and biases. As an anecdote, a friend of mine went to lunch with a handful of other women attorneys at a private business club. One of the male partners came over to their table and said, "Hello ladies, whose birthday are you celebrating?"

Other colleagues shared stories of fighting for equal pay or warding off inappropriate flirting. I never experienced this. My renumeration was tied to performance and no one made unwanted advances.

I wondered whether it would have been different if I had taken a more traditional career path or if I were thin.

I fought for respect, regardless of my gender, always focused on keeping balance as I continued to climb that precarious ladder, determined to get to the top.

Mark and I had not taken our first paycheck yet when, on a hot, humid July night, my world shifted. Curled up in the corner of our living room sofa, I was scanning through channels looking for something to watch on TV. The boys were away at summer camp, and I had just checked on Jackie, who was asleep in her turquoise and pink wallpapered bedroom. I don't remember precisely what I said to my husband—something mundane about upcoming dinner plans or the like—when seemingly out of nowhere he replied, "I want a divorce."

I heard the words but could not process the implication.

I should have been prepared. I had known that the marriage was suffering but I never thought of divorce as an option—we had a family. When my husband and I stopped confiding in one another, I blamed it on our hectic lives; when affection waned, I figured that's what happens after three kids; and I justified our escalating arguments as "par for the course."

Once again, this time louder, he said, "I want a divorce."

"NO!" I screamed, clinging to the arm of the sofa, as if I were riding one of those elevators from the garment district. This time, however, the cable snapped, and it was plummeting right through the ground.

"NO!" "NO!"

What had I done?

What will I do?

I went into Mark's office the next day and dragged the nicked wooden armchair closer to his desk. Knowing that my partner was skittish when it came to emotions, I tried to contain a rush of tears as I said, "I'm getting divorced."

I dug into the bottom of my purse for a tissue and added, "Money is going to be an issue."

Silence. Then he asked, "Do you want to go back to practicing law? That way, at least, you'll have a salary that you can count on."

I thought back to myself as a Girl Scout in Miami going door-to-door. "No. I'd rather sell cookies," I said, adding, "We're going to make this business work."

Desperate to stay with our fledgling business but in need of cash, I put our house on the market. I didn't know what else to do. But when prospective buyers rummaged through my medicine cabinets, poked their heads into my closets, and inventoried my refrigerator, I had a visceral reaction. My children already lost the security of an intact family. How could I let them also lose the security of their childhood home?

In the past, like when my father refused to take me to that business dinner or when I flunked fat camp, pain and shame had caused me to retreat. This time, however, was different; my children's wellbeing was at stake.

I gathered every past hurt, rejection, and abandonment as if they were chips of dry wood and lit them on fire. As the flame roared, I swore, with a Scarlet O' Hara-like declaration of passion, *I will never fall victim again.* I'd accept my role in the destruction of the marriage and move on. We had some good years together and raised three amazing children, but we probably should never have married. I had allowed my need for love to compromise my judgment. It didn't work out for me the way it had for my mother when she married my father.

Whatever it took, I'd make the business succeed. To anyone who had doubted me, mostly to myself, I'd prove my worth and provide a life rich with options for my children.

9

Am I a Good Mother Spreadsheet

DESPITE MY DECLARATION to succeed in business, I still had to cope with an excruciating emptiness in my personal life. It thrust me into the claws of loneliness, a far too familiar state. I would walk in circles around the house, listen to sad music, and gorge on sugar-laced glazed doughnuts and salty, crunchy chips. I knew that I was near bottom when one weekend, hoping to snap me out of my funk, a girlfriend convinced me to go with her to Atlantic City. After checking into our rooms, we raced outside and rented bikes to enjoy the crisp temperature and clear skies of an early winter day. Pedaling south on the boardwalk, I took in the aroma of hotdogs, mustard, catsup, and relish; the stores hawking t-shirts with arrows pointing toward one another saying, "I'm with Stupid" and "Stupid;" and the two-story mall that jutted out into the ocean. When I rode by a beggar, a greasy haired, toothless man wearing torn jeans and a dirt-splotched army jacket, our eyes met, and he smiled. And for a revolution of my tires, I thought, *I wonder if he's single. Should I stop and pursue him*? Instead, I gave him a five-dollar bill.

For the last seventeen years, my ex's family, all Baltimoreans, had embraced me into their lives. We had July 4th barbecues at his sister-in-law's house and Mother's Day brunches at his parents' house. On Saturday nights we went to movies and dinners with his best friends and their wives. Now, these same people had to choose sides. I remained close with a few of his friends, but when it came to family, blood won.

For fleeting moments, I considered taking the kids and moving back to Miami. That way I'd be near my parents, my sister, and my brother. I could look up old high-school friends and cousins. The fantasy was compelling, but it was just that—a fantasy. I couldn't separate my children from their father.

One night, unable to fall asleep, I caught up on my newspapers. An advertisement for a support group for people going through separation and divorce caught my eye. *I am one of them,* I thought, *what do I have to lose?* A week later I attended a meeting that was held in a Jewish Community Center board room. Sitting around the horseshoe table, I surveyed the group of nine—two men and seven women. We became close friends, spending lonely Saturday nights and empty Sunday afternoons together. Bonding with a promise—"You can call me any time day or night and I'll be there for you"—these friends saved me.

I also threw myself into work.

During this time, we had our first big business break. A multi-state law firm called us for a dozen attorneys to help with due diligence—rummaging through boxes of documents looking for privileged communications. They gave us short notice, but we took the challenge. This was a chance to prove ourselves. We would send them our best applicants, and hopefully gain a long-term client. By then we had hired a placement counselor and she put together an impressive team for the job but was one attorney short. Not wanting to let the client down, I flipped through the files. Finding an impressive resume, I said to the counselor, "What's wrong with her?"

"She's getting married on Saturday," she replied.

Without pausing I said, "The interview is 9 a.m., what time is the wedding?"

The counselor got the message, and although she did not send the bride-to-be, she found someone else for the job.

The firm was impressed, and our reputation grew. Within a few months we began to draw salaries. I called my realtor. "I've changed my mind. Please take the house off the market." I thought, *I'm going to do this. I'm really going to do this.*

Years later, as a keynote speaker for a women's business group, I spoke about the importance of adhering to our goals. "Your goal is your destination. Any hurdles that you experience are only detours. Work around them, but never give up. For example, if you live in New York and you're driving to San Francisco, the roads may be fraught with closures, traffic jams, and accidents. You might have to change routes, but, no matter what, you simply view them as annoyances and stay fixed on that final destination."

I never questioned our destination—to become an industry leader. There were, of course, numerous hurdles and challenges involving both work and family: Could Andy's sore throat be strep? Should I cancel an out-of-town trip just in case? How was I going to meet a client's deadline for a team of litigators who were willing to travel to a remote site for a long-term project? What was the deadline for signing Danny up for little league? Why couldn't we find the right manager for the Boston office? Where do I buy ballerina shoes and tights for Jackie? Would we complete a software upgrade in time for a national presentation?

Nevertheless, I loved every minute of it. I hired a part-time graduate student to take the kids to after-school activities, clean the house, food shop, and attend to other needs. I joked to my girlfriends, "Husbands may come and go but a good nanny must last forever."

If that Atlantic City trip was near bottom, I hit bedrock when my children went to their father's apartment as per our custody schedule: one Friday, one Saturday, and one full weekend a month. They also had dinner with him on Tuesdays and Thursdays.

I think back to the first time that he pulled his car into the driveway, honked the horn, and waited for the kids to pile in for a weekend visitation. Dragging their small suitcases, the boys turned to kiss me goodbye, then walked hand-in-hand to their father's car. They buckled their seatbelts. I clung to my daughter. My hands refused to relax and let her go. My ex had to extricate her from my arms and into his own—my baby girl, too young to comprehend my despair. Hysterical, I turned away to shield my anguish from the kids and retreated into the childless silence of home with its neatly made beds, clutter-free floors, and no "what's for dinner?"

Although my children were only with their father for short periods of time, I knew that there were now pieces of their lives that I would not share: laughing at a spoon-on-the-nose competition while eating homemade lasagna; a middle-of-the-night sore throat with my "it will be all right" and a measured dose of liquid Tylenol. When they'd return home, I'd bask in their presence while consumed with dread over their next absence.

My ex was a good father and the children needed to spend time with him. I was confident in his love for them and their love for him, but that didn't ease my emptiness. His judgment wasn't always my judgment, and his values were not always my values.

I added divorce to the liability side of my "Am I a Good Mother" spread sheet.

That kind of guilt never disappears. It merely dissipates.

Decades later, on a vivid fall day, the leaves had turned to shades of yellow, red, and orange. The sky was the blue of my brother's eyes, and the temperature was such that I fluctuated between wearing my sweater or tying it around my waist. Thanksgiving would be here soon.

Monitoring my tone to hide desperation, one-by-one, I called my grown kids and asked, "Do you know what you're doing for the holiday this year?"

Like me, they tried to maintain neutrality in their voices

as they wrestled with the Solomonic guilt of where to spend Thanksgiving—with me, their father, or their spouses' families.

"Let me think about it and get back to you," they replied.

"That's great, whatever you decide is fine," I lied.

Please come home—I want you around my table.

10

Love Before the First Bite

"DESCRIBE YOUR IDEAL man," Patti said, pulling up an armchair in front of my desk.

My ideal man? No one had ever asked me that. Growing up I thought I'd be lucky if *any* man would have me.

I leaned back in my desk chair, closed my eyes, and let my fantasies run wild.

"He has to be smart and funny. A mensch—someone with good character and high morals. Of course, he has to love kids. And I'd love someone who is tall and at least a little overweight." I was still stitching my ego together from the divorce and wanted a man whose girth would quell my insecurities about my own weight.

Patti was Mark's sister. She'd come to visit him at our office. Single herself, she had her finger on the pulse of the dating scene. Digesting my description, she thought for a moment and said, "I know someone. He is an insurance broker that I met when he tried to sell me a policy. He asked me out on a date but he wasn't my type. He's a great guy though. No kids and he's been divorced for a long time."

"Tell me more," I said.

"Wait, he advertises to the legal community." She ruffled through the periodicals on our reception desk then said, "Here's his picture!"

I took the magazine from her hand and looked into a round, smiling face partially covered by a beard. Big blue eyes seemed to stare through my pain. I felt like it was bashert, Yiddish for meant to be.

"Please, give him my phone number."

It turned out that this friend of Patti's, Charles, was away on a cruise. But a few weeks later, when the kids were at their father's we had our first date. I opened my front door to a six-foot, one-inch tall, teddy-bear of a man. With those sparkling eyes, salt and pepper hair, and an easy laugh, I was instantly attracted to him. His full-faced smile drew me in; later, his crushing hugs made me stay. And he was fat—fatter than me.

We sat side-by-side in a booth at his favorite Italian restaurant. The maître d' lingered at our table schmoozing with Charles about local politics while scoping me out. As we sipped our drinks and picked at fried calamari, I asked him, "Why didn't your first marriage work-out?"

Charles put down his scotch and leaned back in his chair, choosing his words deliberately so as not to disparage his ex, "We had different wants and needs. We were married for less than three years; it was better to end things before we had children."

By the time we got to the garlic bread and pasta, I had learned that his blue eyes twinkled when he flirted; he unapologetically delighted in food and drink; and he was funny as well as brilliant. On the way home, when he suggested a stop at Baskin Robbins for chocolate mint ice cream—I was in love before the first bite.

I was thirty-nine years old and had not dated since college. I dreaded releasing my flabby stomach and rear from the tight-fitting jeans that contained them, my breasts from an uplifting underwire bra. But desire won over nerves. While Charles was in the bathroom, I turned off all the lights and dove under the covers with unprecedented speed and agility. I tried to remain calm by steadying my breath as I waited for him to return to the bedroom.

When he finally walked in, he was carrying a small black suitcase. This seemed odd. I knew I was out of the modern dating loop but still didn't think men brought overnight cases with them the first time they had sex.

Charles turned to me sheepishly and said, "Where is the closest outlet?" I looked at him questioningly as he went on to explain, "I need to plug in my CPAP machine."

When it was time to go to sleep, he covered his face with a Darth Vader-type oxygen mask more appropriate for a toxic waste site than a bedroom. It had a long, clear, plastic hose that connected the mask to the machine. It was the early 1990s and CPAP machines were just coming into their own, they were big and bulky, not the small, silent devices in use today. I had never seen one before, not even on TV.

Charles' mortification filled the room. I pinched the skin on my arm to keep from laughing. Then I wrapped my arms around his chest and whispered, "It's okay, it doesn't matter." And thought *I want you, and your machine, to stay with me forever.*

The only comment he made about my over-sized body was, "You're beautiful."

Two years later we were married.

Initially I was reluctant, more accurately humiliated, to don a wedding dress, walk down the aisle, and have a party for the second time—I was the mother of three children. But Charles had pleaded, "This is going to be the happiest day in my life. Please wear a wedding gown for me—I want the whole shebang."

Self-consciously, I visited dozens of bridal shops searching for gowns sized twenty that were beige and simple. I finally found what I was looking for in the plus-size section of a local department store.

Five-year-old Jackie was the flower girl. She wore a white lace dress, black patent-leather shoes, and her hair was held together on top of her head with a white bow. She walked down the aisle tossing petals from side to side—exactly like instructed.

I stood with fifteen-year-old Danny on my left and Andy, twelve, on my right. Dressed in black tuxedoes they guided me towards Charles who waited under the Chuppah flanked by his two best friends. When his eyes met mine, he gave me one of his full-faced grins that made me feel like I was a prize. Afterwards, rather than an elegant extravaganza like my first wedding, we hosted a brunch for family and friends and danced in a circle to the traditional hora.

Charles quickly found his footing in our new family. A man who adores children and animals, he fell head over heels in love with mine. He scored tickets to an All-Star game for the boys and spent hours playing Candy Land with Jackie. Yet he was mindful that they were the progeny of another. He put their father first, accepting that he would always be second. He never experienced the first wobbly steps of a twelve-month-old, or the proud cry of a toddler announcing, "I made poop on the potty." He was relegated to the far chair at parent-teacher conferences and received the last hug at graduations. He celebrated Father's Day with the kids on Mondays, yet never showed signs of jealousy. Rather, he freed the children to love both him and their father without guilt—the ultimate manifestation of love.

Seemingly against all odds, this Rubenesque woman with three children had found a man, a mensch, who cherished us all.

11

Sharing Vulnerabilites

STANDING IN THE lobby of a towering building, I gave the security guard the required information for access to the executive floor. My heart was pounding. After six months of rejections, a head honcho of this Fortune 500 company had finally agreed to a meeting.

During that first year, our start-up had caught on as a cost-effective alternative to traditional staffing for the legal community. We had assembled an impressive cadre of attorneys and implemented a software system to help us match the credentials of the lawyers with the requirements of the job. Whatever the client's needs, we provided them highly vetted candidates in a timely manner. For example: a small firm requested an experienced litigator to step in while their associate was on maternity leave; the legal department of a manufacturing business required a team of entry-level lawyers for a due diligence review; and a multi-city defense firm asked for an aviation attorney who could speak Mandarin.

The most important aspect of my job was sales. I kept a running list of the major "players" in the legal community and tried to arrange in-person meetings. I highlighted those prospective clients who had the potential to generate significant revenue. This particular client was near the top of my list with a prominent red star next to their name. In preparation for my presentation, I researched their mission, rate of growth, public records of litigation, and outside counsel.

Once the uniformed security officer cleared me, he called up to the director's office. Her assistant came downstairs to escort me to the executive suite. I straightened my back, put a smile on my face, and offered my hand for a shake to a petite, red-headed women in her fifties wearing a tailored St. John skirt and jacket. After exchanging the normal pleasantries, I glanced toward her desk. On the corner, I spied a Weight Watcher's point counter.

"Do you count points?" I asked.

"Yes, for several months and I've lost ten pounds."

If that was the case, I thought, she must be at her goal weight. She was skinny.

I had recently joined Weight Watchers—again. Self-conscious of my own need to lose ten pounds several times over, I said, "So do I!"

She invited me to join her for lunch in the private dining room that was attached to her office. We each ordered a niçoise salad and discussed diets, calories, and the challenges of finding the time to shop and prepare healthy meals while working full time. The more we talked, the more we revealed. I found myself opening up about my divorce. She talked about the illness of a close friend. Pretense lifted and we settled into a real conversation about other challenges that face working women. Of course, we also discussed her business needs and I explained why our company would surpass her expectations.

A week later I learned that we were awarded their business. I was ecstatic. This account gave us another notch on our belt of credibility and the confidence to pursue contracts with other mammoth organizations.

How ironic that my greatest insecurity allowed me to form a relationship that would help me reach the highest levels of success. By exposing my vulnerabilities, I had implicitly given this client permission to share her own. She did not have to be perfect around me. She did not have to pretend or meet all of those superficial expectations. This experience changed me in a powerful and significant way. I was no longer afraid to be authentic in forming hundreds of precious business relationships. Over the years I shared, appropriately, the travails of divorce, the fight over body image, and the guilt of a working mom.

I thought back to those shapely women in the dressing room who criticized their bodies when I had worked in retail. I also replayed the words of self-incrimination that I heard from women clients and colleagues throughout my career. *I can't believe this humidity; I don't want to give my presentation with frizzy hair. I'm not pretty enough to work in sales. I'm not sophisticated enough to accept a promotion to the New York office.* I wondered, why are women so hard on themselves? Why do we focus on our imperfections rather than on our strengths?

For way too many years, shame over my body had consumed me. I believed that my pudgy physique rendered me powerless and insignificant. I was not alone with my insecurities, but it was time to try to let them go.

MY PARENTS HAD stopped to visit us in Baltimore on their way to Atlantic City. My mother was getting her hair done that morning, so I said to my father, "Rather than staying home by yourself, why don't you come with me. Mark and I are meeting with a well-known franchise lawyer to explore the possibility of issuing licenses. I think you'll find it interesting."

My father had never seen me operate in my environment. I thought back to all those times that I followed on his heels at the gun business. It felt good to reverse our roles. I hoped he'd be impressed. Perhaps he'd even look at me with some respect.

The conference room was not much different than the many I had visited throughout my career. An extra-long, dining room-like table and black leather chairs on wheels filled the dark-paneled, rectangular space. Screens hung at one end for presentations, and in the corner was a cart laden with coffee, water, sodas, and snacks.

Dad sat at the far end of the table. He didn't offer an opinion or ask a question as Mark, our lawyer, and I discussed the pros and cons of franchising: on the one hand it was a road to rapid expansion; on the other, we'd be granting territorial licenses to someone who might not perform to expectations.

"So, what did you think?" I asked my father as we rode down the elevator and exited the building.

"I don't know anything about franchising. But I'm sure, whatever route you take, you'll do fine. Mom should be done with the beauty parlor by now so I better be going."

I would have liked more from him, but this time I did not feel defeated. While we ultimately rejected the franchise route because we did not want to give up control, we were determined to expand. We had set our sights on opening offices in every major city throughout the country. In this way, if a client from DC had a matter in Chicago, we could send them a team of local attorneys to meet their staffing needs.

I was incredibly driven. Business opportunities and challenges consumed me. I created advertising campaigns while showering in the morning and dreamt about acquisition targets overnight. The business continued to explode.

Multiple staffing companies reached out to us to inquire about acquisition. We hired consultants and met with corporate suitors who wined and dined us, wooing us with charm and money. I still remember the president of one potential acquirer calling me to say, "I'm not sure we want to get married, but we certainly want to be invited to the dance." For the first time in my life, I was pursued. Actively. Charles had fallen in love with my essence; these corporate bigwigs with my profit potential. My business acumen was more seductive to them than dress size. Although long, sexy legs and a firm butt to match would not have hurt my chances, I finally understood that physical beauty alone did not lead to success. Rather, it was ambition, determination, and confidence that opened those doors. How unfortunate that nobody had given me that message – that I wasted years in self-loathing over that which didn't matter.

Less than three years after I had first marketed myself out to take those depositions, Mark and I sold the business. "Why did you want to sell?" asked a friend.

I tried to explain. "I learned from watching my mother gamble, if you stay too long at the table, you might lose. I want to take my winnings and play with someone else's money. It's not that I'm going to leave. My partner and I will stay on and lead this company to national dominance – but without personal financial risk."

On the way to the settlement, I called my father. I heard him say, "Make sure you get options," but the call dropped, as I was pulling my car into the parking garage, before he could elaborate. Mark and I, along with a team of attorneys, balanced stacks of papers and legal pads as we ironed out the final sticking points of the acquisition.

We had agreed on almost all the points when I asked, "What about options?"

"What about them?" said the acquirer.

I kept silent.

"How many do you want?"

I had no idea. At the time, I didn't know what an option was.

"What do you think is fair?" I answered.

He threw out a number. Thinking back to my father's business lessons, I said, "Don't insult me. Give me a real number."

He doubled it.

"You're getting closer," I said.

He threw out his final offer.

"You've got a deal."

Much later I would understand the value of what I had negotiated. At the time I was focused on the sale price. The dollars made me dizzy with pride. As soon as the deal was finalized, I left the conference room and walked two blocks to an ATM. The attorneys had assured us that monies were transferred, but I needed to see it for it to be real. I slid my card in the slot, punched in my code, and hit the "balance inquiry" button. There it was—I walked back to work with my head held higher than a beauty queen contestant in her sash and crown.

12

Brains and Beauty

STANDING AT THE door of the mammoth, white, concrete building, my body shook, my heart pounded, and I feared the onset of
an anxiety attack. I inhaled and exhaled to the count of four—a
technique that helped steady me throughout the years. Meeting
that director of human resources was child's play compared to
the courage it took for me to walk into the gym.

During my yearly physical, my internist had said to me,
"Laura, you're in your forties. If you don't start exercising and
eating healthily, you're looking at dire consequences: diabetes,
high blood pressure, heart disease, and orthopedic issues to
name a few." For the first time in my life, I was motivated to get
in shape for the right reason—my health.

After consummating the sale of our business, we had entered
a period of rapid growth. Mark and I stayed on as incentivized
employees, heading the legal staffing arm of the acquiring con-
glomerate as President and CEO, respectively. We plunged into
achieving our goal of establishing a presence in major cities
throughout the country. In this way we would dominate the now
rapidly growing market for temporary legal staffing.

We hired additional staff, pursued acquisitions, and retained
a realtor to locate a corporate site. He showed us an ideal space,
the right square footage and price, in an office building located
off of the beltway. It was also right next door to this gym. With

my doctor's warning reverberating, I said, "Let's take it." Now I'd have no excuses. *If Mohammed can't go to the mountain, the mountain would come to Mohammed.*

Once we settled into our new offices, I made the appointment. Trying to comply with the receptionist's instructions, "Come dressed to work-out," I went into our office restroom and wriggled into a pair of black Lycra shorts. I pulled an oversized black t-shirt over my head and sat on the toilet to put on white ankle socks and a pair of extra-wide tennis shoes.

The gym was a cavernous space with high ceilings and rows of exercise machines. A leotarded membership counselor guided me through collections of treadmills, exercise bikes (some that required the use of both arms and legs), ellipticals, and stair climbers. She said there was a "one hour time limit" on some of the more popular torture devices. *An hour*, I thought, a *whole hour–I couldn't last for fifteen minutes.*

There were multiple rooms for classes: yoga, Pilates, and some kind of dancing with jazz. I was perspiring just from the tour. "Wait until you see the locker room," the counselor said with a lilt I already disdained. I followed her into the door marked "Women" and immediately wanted to bolt. Ladies of all ages were walking around in various stages of undress. Some were without bras, others with no panties, many wrapped in towels, and a few completely nude–but none of them seemed to care. I cared. I felt like a creepy voyeur.

I was glad that I had changed in the office bathroom; no one would catch me prancing around in my birthday suit. I thought back to those South Florida models and wannabes flaunting bikini-clad perfection–perhaps this wasn't for me.

As the saleswoman pointed out the amenities included with membership, such as blow dryers, straightening irons, and make-up mirrors, I forced myself to settle down. Then I took another look at those women. While some looked better than others, nobody was perfect. I couldn't help but notice cottage-cheese butts, cellulite-pocked thighs, and flat chests—the most admirable trait in the room was attitude.

Attitude. Now, that was something I had.

When we returned to the sales office, I committed to an annual membership.

I stuck with that gym and before long I realized that nobody paid attention to my appearance, or if they did, they didn't seem to care. I batted away my self-consciousness and paid extra for a personal trainer to keep me on track. I met with her twice a week for an hour of weightlifting plus the treadmill or bike to elevate my heart rate.

I tried to eat mostly healthy foods and stayed away from processed sugars and white starches. I was not perfect. There were slips and binges. The biggest difference between that time and all my previous failures was forgiveness—I gave myself permission for imperfection. Rather than focusing on how I screwed up, which inevitably led to a three-month pig-out, I'd start fresh the next morning. I kept reminding myself that, *this is a way of life, not a diet.*

I lost forty pounds. While I was not thin—a size twelve or fourteen—I could finally fit into the clothes that lined the racks of the women's stores I had once managed.

It turned out that when I satiated my ego with business success the need to fill my stomach lessened. I had desperately needed to be accepted as me, regardless of my weight. Once that happened, the extra pounds became irrelevant, and I could finally let them go.

I explored plastic surgery to get rid of the hanging skin leftover from my weight loss and made an appointment with a prominent plastic surgeon for an evaluation. His nurse handed me a string belt with a small paper triangle in the middle. In a stern voice she instructed, "Take everything off and put this on." A few minutes later she returned with the doctor and asked me to stand on an elevated wooden block. The doctor took in every fat-filled crevice of my body. He did not try to assuage my humiliation but simply muttered and shook his head as he encircled me with a camera snapping pictures of my flab.

After I put my business clothes back on, the nurse ushered me into the doctor's office. He handed me an album filled with pictures of other flawed patients: A woman whose breasts hung down to her waist on one page, on the opposite page the same women displaying new perky peaks. Another set of pictures showed the before and after of a woman with a prominent turkey neck. I ran my hand under my own chin and thought, *maybe this will work*. Finally, the doctor fed my paper-triangled covered body into his computer and amplified my flaws (which did not need magnification).

With a practiced exuberance, as if he had won the plastic surgery lottery, he said, "Now, with the help of imaging, you can see what you will look like once we complete several (painful) procedures." With bated breath I stared at the screen. There I was, minus most of my fat. But it was still me. If I walked past a crowded construction sight, heads would not turn. There would be no whistles or shouts of "hey babe, whatcha doing tonight?

I rejected the surgery, and in so doing still stood firmly on the brains team of that brains/beauty war. In refusing this extreme medical procedure, I made a deliberate decision once and for all to no longer subject myself to the mindless adherence of arbitrary rules.

Would I have gone through with it for a guarantee of better results, if the outcome promised to turn me into the diva of that long-ago birthday wish? It would depend on the surgical risk—but probably.

On the other hand, I would not have agreed to an instant ride to the top. I would not have wanted to miss out on the climb. I thrived on every nuance that took me up a rung: winning a new client, opening a new location, providing a new service. Likewise, if that same grantor of wishes offered to take twenty of my unwanted pounds in trade for twenty points of IQ—I would have given him an unequivocal, "NO."

Mercifully, we no longer must pick teams—it is no longer an either/or. Beauty is subjective, dependent on cultural norms (both internal and external). The latter without the former is meaningless. Likewise, there are many types of intelligence: emotional, linguistic, philosophical, and common sense, to name a few.

When I was growing up, the worth of a man was measured by his success, a woman's by her beauty. I was not born with the second, so I put every ounce of my being into achieving the first. It took a lifetime for me to fully understand that the concept was fallacious. Worth is measured by character and deeds of kindness—not by what we take, but by what we leave.

FOR A WHILE, Charles stood on the sidelines and watched me lose weight. But I worried about his health and convinced him to join the same gym. Charles is an all or nothing kind of guy, and before I knew it, he was hooked. Rather than exercising twice a week like me, he began lifting weights and doing sit-ups daily. My big bear morphed into a buff Adonis. And I hated it.

We were at a neighborhood holiday party when one of our friends said, "Hi, Laura, you look great," and then, "Charles, wow, you look amazing. How'd you lose so much weight?"

While my once fettuccine alfredo loving husband proselytized about "portion control" and "barbell squats," I slinked off to find a drink. Waiting for my Sauvignon Blanc, I flashed back to the time Charles and I ravaged a giant éclair in the car on our way to buy our first treadmill.

In the parking lot of "Bodies R Us" (or something similarly sounding), we finished the entire twelve-inch, custard-filled pastry. Still licking fudge off our fingers, a Hulk Hogan look-alike approached, eyed us up and down, and asked, "So, what are your goals for a treadmill?"

I replied, "Do you have a napkin I can use to wipe my hands?" Charles and I broke into hysterical laughter.

I yearned for those days.

Through those early years, our bond and waistlines thickened. We snuggled under the covers with double-stuffed Oreos and peanut M&Ms. We watched the Miami Marathon from front row seats at a little French restaurant. We snickered at the runners who favored perspiration and shortness-of-breath over cheese-filled omelets and buttery croissants slathered with apricot jam.

We had also shared the humiliation of being fat in a world that extolled thinness. We suffered raised eyebrows when we reached for a second hot roll, smirks as we wedged our derrieres into airplane seats, and giggles when we pulled down walking shorts that stuck to our thighs.

It was us against them—a united front that deepened our connection and lessened our self-consciousness.

His stint at the gym eventually turned into what felt like outright treason—he began counting calories. "Honey, at lunch today instead of a Big Mac I ordered a small hamburger. Guess how many calories I saved?" I thought, *good for you and I don't care.* I knew he had officially switched teams when he replaced his usual 'big man stack' of pancakes drenched in butter and syrup, with a short stack and a "sugar-free syrup, please" to the waitress. Even worse, he traded in his "Drinks Well with Friends" t-shirt for a clingy Under Armour.

When we went out to dinner and our waiter asked, "How about dessert?" before I had a chance to respond, Charles patted his (now flat) stomach and said, "None for me." When he said this, I wanted to smash his diet in the face. Not only had he crossed over to the svelte team, but he'd become the captain.

Had he become my parents?

I had finally made peace with my body. But now that Charles was in shape, would I have to cut my calories even more and increase my workouts to daily sweat sessions that offered no room for the forgiveness I'd learned to extend to myself?

Weighted down by my anxieties, I went to my husband and

confessed my fears. He took me in his arms and whispered, "I love you just the way you are."

Together we renegotiated our affair with exercise. We took long walks, swam, and went bike riding. When we joined my brother and sister-in-law for a long weekend in Monterey, I experienced that endorphin high which, up until then, I'd only read about. We rented bikes and pedaled along that glorious 17-mile drive on the Monterey Peninsula. I took in the majesty of the Pacific Ocean, mesmerized by the sea lions and seals slithering up and down the rocks. The wind whipped through my hair as I gawked at the mansions. I was present, in the moment. I was my best me. I felt such gratitude that I could pedal and balance the bike. I shouted to Charles and my brother and sister-in-law, "I'm passing on the right."

I pedaled faster and faster—incrimination, accusation, and toxicity fell in my wake. Not sure where I was headed, but triumphant in what I'd left behind.

13

Maternal Guilt

I STUCK MY head into Andy's room and said, "Come down for dinner. We're eating early tonight so that you can go trick-or-treating."

"Did you get my Incredible Hulk costume?" he asked.

I closed my eyes and thought, *I can't believe I forgot to buy his costume.* With everything that was going on at work (we were full steam into escalating profits and market domination), it had slipped my mind. Another debit on my "Am I a Good Mother?" spread sheet.

"Oh honey, I forgot. I'm so sorry. But no problem, I'll go the store right now and be home before you're done with dinner."

When I got to the drugstore, the shelves were bare except for a few witches, princesses, and a hobo.

I wanted to fold into myself and disappear. I had let my son down.

I came home with the hobo costume, and with a forced enthusiasm I said, "Isn't this great!"

"I don't want to be a hobo—I want to be a superhero." He launched into full meltdown mode.

In that moment, I would have paid anything for *any* hero costume: Batman, Superman, or, his favorite, the Incredible Hulk. It was late, though, and the stores were closing. There was nothing I could do. In a last-ditch effort I offered, "We can get a sheet, cut holes for your eyes, and you can be a ghost."

He looked down at his dirty tennis shoes and replied, "I guess I'll be a hobo."

Then there was the time that I had an early flight to meet with a client to iron out details of a large staffing project. On my way out the door, Lisa, our nanny, who was driving Jackie to school that morning, called me and said, "We're okay. Jackie is fine. But someone rammed into me, and the ambulance is on the way."

"Where are you, exactly?" I asked, already panicking.

I drove to the site and found my daughter on a stretcher with her neck in a brace as medics loaded her into the ambulance. Lisa was immobilized on her own cot.

I leaned over Jackie's precious face, tears streaming down my own, and asked "Are you okay?"

"I'm fine, Mom," said my brave little girl.

It turned out that our nanny had hurt her hip, which had absorbed the force of braking when she tried to lessen the impact of the crash, and she needed surgery. Eventually, she was okay. Jackie, true to her word, was fine.

I cancelled my business meeting from the emergency room at the hospital. The accident was the fault of a distracted driver. By reacting quickly, Lisa had minimized the consequences, and yet, I thought, *that's what you get for hiring someone else to drive your daughter to school.*

Another time there was a field trip to New York for Jackie's class and their parents. All year, Jackie had looked forward to traipsing with her friends to see the Statue of Liberty and the Empire State Building. I had a conflict with work that I could not rearrange, so I sent Danny, who was nineteen at the time, in my place. Charles and I met up with them that evening and, to assuage my guilt, I overpaid for tickets to see *The Lion King* on Broadway.

Did Mufasa, Simba, and Nala compensate for my absence on the tour? I'll never really know. Would I have remembered Andy's costume if I weren't working? Not sure. And would that same driver have hit the car if I were the one at the wheel? Most likely.

The earnings from my career provided opportunities for my children. They went to sleep-away camps with their friends, trekked through Disney World, sailed on cruises, and attended the colleges of their choice. Yet, as I first reflected when pregnant with Danny, my guilt was stoked in knowing that had we not needed the money, I would have still chosen to work.

In retrospect, like most mothers, I was too hard on myself. When Halloween costumes and field trips fell through the cracks of business responsibilities, I went directly to self-blame. And that wasn't fair. Although I had gone "all in" to both careering and parenting, I had never equalized the importance of the two. I would have sold those cookies door-to-door for the rest of my life before compromising the well-being of my children. I would have tossed every penny I ever earned into the ocean for a guarantee of their health. I would have extricated the nails from my fingertips to ensure their happiness. Guilt served as a reminder of my priorities, and like the lipstick in my purse, although I wasn't always focused on it, it was always there.

A journal entry to my children reads:

> *I pray that you never equate the amount of time I spend with you to the amount of love I have for you.*
>
> *I pray you do not feel the limits of my availability but learn from me that possibility has no limits.*
>
> *I pray you do not feel neglected when I fail to oversee your homework and learn from the responsibility how to oversee your life.*
>
> *I pray you understand that while I'm attending to dozens of other matters, nothing ever matters as much as you.*
>
> *I pray my choices give you permission to lead your life to the fullest rather than filling your life trying to meet the choices of others.*
>
> *Most of all, I pray that I am right.*

LIKE THAT FIRST time after the divorce, I still felt eviscerated whenever the kids were with their father for long weekends and summer trips. Reaching for distraction, one summer weekend Charles suggested, "Let's go to the beach."

We drove three hours to Ocean City, Maryland, and checked into a hotel room with a balcony overlooking the water. The next morning, Charles put on a pair of navy-blue swim trunks while I changed into black bathing suit shorts and a T-shirt. We rented an umbrella and beach chairs. Charles opened his book, and I stared out to sea.

I couldn't sit still. I reached into my beach bag and pulled out my earphones and iPod. I tuned into a 1960s classic rock station and walked north. Sand nestled between my toes and humidity frizzed my hair.

The movement of the currents lulled me into a calm. Slowly, I released bits of the shame over my role in the divorce, guilt for being a working mother, other regrets of the past, and the endless planning for tomorrows. I felt, in a good way, irrelevant—a mere particle in the vastness of the universe.

From that point on, we spent our childless days at the beach. At first, I went to avoid my void, then later, to embrace contentment. Within a year we bought a small condo overlooking the blue waters of the sea. I chose lemon yellow for the walls, a marbleized grey ceramic tile for the floors. On the shelves over my desk, I arranged books from my favorite authors: Joan Didion, Pearl Buck, and Anne Tyler.

I placed knick-knacks on tables (mostly carvings of pudgy women). And I hung paintings of Botero's voluptuous ladies on my walls. This was my way of reminding myself, *you don't have to be thin to be beautiful.*

Over time, those long beach walks provided perspective. Although I never stopped missing my kids when they were with their father, I learned to accept that time away from them was an unintended consequence of divorce. Acceptance brought peace.

The moments of contentment expanded into hours. I'd continue to play my music and walk for miles and miles, forgetting where I'd come from, oblivious to where I was going, but satisfied being where I was. And blissfully ignorant of the feelings of irrelevancy that awaited around the corner.

PART III

WITHOUT A BUSINESS CARD WHO AM I?

14

An Empty Tube of Toothpaste

IN UNDER TEN years, through continued internal growth, acquisitions, and cold starts, our two-person business had grown into a mammoth industry leader.

I was ready to shed responsibility and pursue new interests and challenges. Mark agreed that we had surpassed our goals and that it was time to move on. Although I experienced moments of angst as to what I'd do next, I was too submerged in earnings, succession planning, and other legal and financial matters to focus on a plan. I wanted to leave the company in stellar shape, and I needed some down time before deciding how to proceed.

Perhaps I should have been better prepared.

The first morning that I awoke without an alarm I went to the bathroom, brushed my teeth, downed two cups of coffee, and panicked. *What do I do now? How will I fill my day, the week, the month? Had I made a mistake? Should I have stayed on?*

I had created a home office in my son Andy's former bedroom. We furnished it with a three-sided, pine desk and an extra-wide black vinyl chair. Charles hooked up the computer, monitor, and printer. Together we went to an office supply store and loaded the shopping cart with silver organizing trays, folders, legal pads, staplers, and a pencil sharpener.

I had nothing to do in that room except pay our bills and surf the internet for ideas that might capture me. It wasn't just about keeping busy; it was about finding purpose. I felt lost and displaced, like a puppy who had wandered too far from its litter. One snowy afternoon, while Charles was at work, the internet shut down just as I was looking into Osher (adult education) classes. Not knowing what to do, I tried unplugging the wire from the router and plugging it back in, but there was still no connection. With the force of a labor contraction, it hit me: without an IT department or administrative assistant how would I manage? And, even worse, manage what?

Anxiety moved in like an unruly tenant that resisted eviction. I went for walks around the neighborhood, but instead of feeling in the moment, I was bored by the sameness. I called friends to chat but had nothing to contribute to the conversation. I cleaned out closets and drawers while musing, *my housekeeper would do a much better job.* When nothing else worked, I went to the beach.

In my lemon-yellow bedroom at the seaside condominium, I awoke to the familiar cacophony of waves kissing the shore before receding towards the horizon. They, like me, flowed without purpose, back and forth, back and forth. Some were mild, and had I walked into their path they would have only reached my ankles. Others were fierce, threatening to send me crashing to the ocean floor.

That morning, inhaling the scents of salt air and sunscreen, I walked two miles north and then retraced my steps to return home. The following day I changed direction and walked south. I replaced my iPod with an iPhone and downloaded my favorite artists. Shuffling between the Three Tenors, Cat Stevens, Bob Dylan, and Carole King, I planted the soles of my feet in the firm sand and trudged forward, one step at a time.

On the last morning, heading north again, I was struck by a bolt of gratitude. How dare I focus on where I was going rather than on all I had achieved? I had climbed to the top of the ladder and gained financial independence, and I became a role model for my children in that respect. I never had to sell my home. In fact, I could afford to I renovate it. Although I had worked hard and was strategic, I knew that much of my success was luck. But as my father always had said, "The harder you work, the luckier you'll become."

Before turning back to our condo, I took one last look out to sea and wondered, *Can I, like the waves, abandon myself to the pull of gravity? Or must I continue to take control and prove my worth?*

DURING THOSE FIRST two years of retirement, I started over a dozen new businesses in my head. I'd call my former partner and say, "I have a great idea."

He'd listen intently, like I was sharing a hot stock tip.

I'd log onto GoDaddy and similar websites to register names for my idea du jour: a company that supplied substitute teachers to school systems; a camp for women to learn confidence; a folding flip-flop that would fit in a pocket for walks on the beach.

Coming up with the ideas and playing them out gave me a rush; thinking of actual execution and implementation killed the buzz. The only way I knew how to be happy was by working. Not the contentment, appreciation, or gratitude kind of happy, but the adrenaline-fueled high that spilled into obsession. The fixation on "what else can we do to make the business grow" gave me a place to put my thoughts. But my drive had waned, and my risk-tolerance had tanked. It wasn't the way it had been before, when I had nothing to lose. And, although I received job offers, I did not want to work for someone else.

I joined boards and volunteered for part-time leadership positions in education, health care, and the Jewish community. I was driven to motivate other women to achieve their career goals. I became a sought-after speaker, and I addressed filled auditoriums with the message that we must bring in business to succeed, and to that end, we have to reach out and form authentic connections with decision makers.

Oftentimes, I shared the story about connecting with that corporate client over our low-calorie lunch. In relating to one another with authenticity, I told them, we form strong connections, develop relationships, and jump-start careers.

One spring evening, I was seated on a panel with two other businesswomen for some sort of "Successful Women Tell All" event. I watched as the moderator shifted her legs into a practiced cross. Her right calf bounced against her left knee causing her skirt to climb up mid-thigh. She brought her mic close to her lips, ran her hand through her wavy, auburn hair and said, "Now for the first question. Laura, I'll start with you. What was your greatest challenge?"

I couldn't and wouldn't compete with this poised, sexy woman. Instead, I decided to practice what I preached and answered, "Getting dressed for work every morning." After the audience's laughter quieted, I went on. "It was hard for me to portray an image of a successful businesswoman when I needed a size eighteen business suit with an elastic waist skirt or pants in case I bloated up after lunch."

More laughter.

"And my extra-wide bunioned feet left me no choice but to wear ugly flats that looked more like boxes than shoes."

When the moderator nervously shook her leg, I felt as if her grey sexy heels were taunting me.

My co-panelists gave the audience more tangible advice about setting goals, rainmaking, and work-life balance, and then it was back to me.

"Who was your mentor or role model?" she asked.

Another softball. I answered, "My father."

There was no one whose approval meant more to me. Had I done enough to compensate for not meeting his standards of what mattered in a woman? Although I had made peace with this issue for myself, it's also true that no matter how old we are, we will always seek approval from our parents.

Maybe it was time to find out.

A few weeks later I flew to Miami and met my parents for breakfast at their favorite deli. When my mother went to the bathroom, I knew this was my chance. My father despised fishing for compliments, so I treaded carefully. "Dad," I asked, "is it weird to you that I sold the business?"

Between forkfuls of eggs, nova, and onions, he said, "No, it's not weird. You did good."

Then he took a swig of his decaffeinated coffee and added, "Don't ever forget whoever you pass on the way up you meet again on the way down."

I leaned forward in the worn, brown leather booth, waiting, longing, for more.

All I got was, "Would you like some of my eggs?"

I took a sip of my coffee and scooped out the insides of my bagel.

He added, "You know, Mom is in awe of you."

My mother was in awe of *me*?

I asked the waiter for light cream cheese.

That night I couldn't fall asleep. I played and replayed his words, *You did good. You did good. Mom is in awe of you.*

And while I wished my mother could have expressed her feelings to me directly, my father's words meant more than that ATM receipt I examined on the day the business was sold.

STANDING IN FRONT of the podium in a synagogue's smallest auditorium, named after a generous donor, I looked out over a group of septuagenarian/octogenarian attendees. Silver-haired women outnumbered the men, who tried to appear dapper in their navy sports jackets, sweaters, and dark suits.

This was not the audience I had expected when the Rabbi invited me to speak about my business journey. I took a sip of water, moved the microphone close to my lips, and thanked everyone for coming. I took in the room and thought that, just like

Caribbean Islands and law firm conference rooms, synagogues look similar to one another with their warm colors, ancient scrolls, Hebrew letters, and hushed whispers. I began a well-rehearsed introduction. "Most human resource departments now understand the advantages of a contingent workforce model. However, that was not the case when we started our business."

A few minutes into my speech, I saw their eyes glazing and heads drooping.

I took another sip of water and paused.

This group was not interested in what I had to say. I wondered why they were here at all. Was it out of curiosity? Perhaps to placate family members who urged them to "get out of the house." I noticed a recently widowed congregant in a wrinkled black suit sitting slumped to the side of his metal folding chair, and another temple member, trying to hide her chemo-induced baldness with a blue paisley scarf, was sipping instant coffee and crunching on potato chips. Her polyester garbed girlfriend on her right looked like she was sleeping, with her eyes closed and the corners of her lips turned upwards into a slight smile.

Then I realized they were here to escape the silence of their now empty lives. I remembered those nursing home residents that I saw while driving with my father when I was a child, and a jolt shot through me, as if I had bitten into an ice cube with an infected tooth.

Was this my future? Would I flock to free presentations on subjects I didn't care about just for something to do?

For a while I had tried to negate my growing unease. While my non-profit work was meaningful, (I raised money to help Jewish causes, I was active on a hospital board, and I was involved with organizations empowering women), it was not enough. I was inspired by what these organizations stood for and grateful for the opportunities to contribute to their success. But I needed more. At the same time, my speaking engagements were no longer as fulfilling. I did not feel the same connection I once had with working mothers. The audiences appeared younger and younger, and I no longer felt relevant. They yearned for soothing stories of work-life balance and inspirational anecdotes on customer acquisition. But I was no longer interested in talking about how to get to the top. Now I wanted to figure out how to climb down. But was this what awaited me once I descended? The thought made me panic—there had to be more. But what?

I awoke from my reverie and looked into the eyes of those senior citizens. I wanted to offer them words of hope and possibility. As I had so many times in my life, I pivoted. "Enough about the business. Let's talk about life after retirement."

I pointed to a member that I knew, "Carl, would you share with us what now gives you meaning and pleasure?"

"My family," he said, so softly that I had to repeat his answer so that the audience could hear.

Looking to engage others I asked, "Would anyone else like to share their thoughts?"

I hoped for a revelation, for words of optimism and encouragement, perhaps more for myself than for my audience.

Finally, a bald man wearing a blue cardigan sweater said, "The instant coffee is lukewarm and muddy."

I thanked everyone for coming and went home.

I have to get better at vetting my audiences, I thought, before pouring myself a glass of wine.

THE AIMLESSNESS INSIDE of me continued to grow. My adult children were waist deep in the "I need space" stages of life and Charles was wrapped up in his work. I felt lost, marginalized. When I got up in the mornings, I felt as though I had lived out my purpose and was no longer needed, or like a pen without ink, an empty tube of toothpaste, entirely disposable. This emptiness grabbed me and simply refused to let go.

The synagogue audience had not provided me with inspiration, and neither could my mother.

We spoke every day. When I voiced my feelings of irrelevance she said, "Laura, you've done enough. Why can't you just relax?"

"Relax? Why would I want to relax?"

My mother's approach to aging terrified me.

While she never worked outside of the home, raising three children and supporting my father's climb to success had filled her early years. Once he retired and we were all married, she had her own brand of emptiness to contend with.

To fill her void, she began playing the slot machines in her late forties. By the time she was in her seventies, she was considered a high stakes gambler. Standing erect, she was a 5-feet, 4-inches tall yet made a striking figure. A former fashionista, she now was relegated to wearing thick, black, orthopedic shoes and a faux-leather fanny pack. Leaning over her walker, she'd shuffle across the casino floor to the high-level slot room. There she'd play dollar and five-dollar machines, three coins at a time, equaling three to fifteen dollars a pull. Sometimes, if she were winning, she'd play the ten-dollar slot machine. When she was on a roll, she was invincible. The minute she left the casino, she'd call me with a play-by-play. I'd take a deep breath, trying to honor her jubilance without reinforcing her addiction.

"You're not going to believe it! I kept watching this machine. I knew it was going to hit. I waited for the man playing it to finally leave then I grabbed it...and...and...it hit!"

"Mom, that's great."

"It's like I have magic fingers, I'm possessed! While I was waiting for the hostess to bring me my check, I played another machine and that one hit too."

"You're on a lucky streak, Mom. But it can turn at any time."

"Can you believe this? I can't believe it. Do you know how much money I now have in my gambling account?"

I didn't know and I didn't care. Whatever money was in her account one day would not be there the next. She had not won the money, she had borrowed it until the next time she lost.

As she babbled on, I didn't want to burst her fantasy with reality. Aging had brought her so many challenges: poor health, a receding social life, and the loss of confidence in performing everyday functions, like driving on the freeway. How could I diminish her exuberance? She could no longer control her ailing body but, when those red sevens aligned, she controlled the world.

The casino's chaotic chatter seemed to drown out the emptiness in her life. She lost herself to the Wheel of Fortune, gleefully succumbing to the ding, ding, ding of the bells. It was more than the jackpots. Although I hate to admit it, she was, like me, seeking purpose. As Queen of the Slots, she assumed an identity. She saw herself as a winner, one who could beat the system. In her own way she had found meaning.

As long as I can remember, my mother had loved to gamble. At first, it was every year or so, when she and my father flew from their home in Miami to vacation in Las Vegas. Then, in the late 1970s, casinos opened in Atlantic City. Every couple of months, my parents drove up to visit me in Baltimore. They stayed for a few days and then hurried on to the Jersey shore. They were escorted to the presidential suite of their casino of choice, where they dropped their luggage and raced to the casino floor. My father would head to the poker room while my mother charged single-mindedly to the slots. She'd embrace her "lucky" machine, caress its handle, and try to seduce it into submission. "Come on baby. You can do it. Do it for me." She was not a faithful lover. If her slot machine did not payout, she tossed it aside and moved on to the next one.

I judged her harshly. Was she buying purpose?

I wrestled with my negativity. I recognized that she had always been generous with all of us. Gambling is what she did for herself. She had stopped traveling, shopping, and entertaining. This was her only real pleasure. It was not my money and not my business.

Only later did I understand why it triggered terror and resentment in me. My mother's adrenaline rush when she won a jackpot was like mine when I made a cunning acquisition or a savvy new hire. I desperately wanted her to be a better role-model, to show me a different kind of happiness.

15

Is Busy the New Rich and Thin?

SIXTY IS THE new *forty. You're only as old as you feel. Age is only a number.* I read everything I could get my hands on about retirement, aging, empty nesting, and related subjects, and I directed all of my energy into figuring out how to proceed with my life.

I sought the advice of other women. I was not discriminating in my selection—whenever and wherever I ran into a woman of a certain age, I questioned her. Like the sixty-something woman with short, streaked hair and a tennis-player build who sat next to me in a nail salon in Miami.

I had just chosen charcoal gray from the wheel of nail polish colors. Although it occurred to me that I no longer needed business appropriate colors (bubble bath pinks, eggshell whites, maroon reds, and grays), it is hard to relinquish markers of an old identity.

I turned to the Billie Jean King wannabe, her fingers soaking in a glass bowl of water, and asked, "Are you a regular here?"

"Yes, we retired to Miami ten years ago."

"So, what's retirement like for you? How do you spend your day?"

She gave me that knowing smile and said, "I wake up in the morning and drink two cups of coffee. Afterward, I plan my lunch. This is the life I promised myself when I retired from the school system, and I love it."

That's it. That's how she spends her day.

I leaned back, as if she were a snake coiled for a bite.

My manicurist was ready to open the jar of gray nail polish. I shook my head and said, "I changed my mind, how about the mulberry purple?"

Other subjects of my interrogation were women who, like my mother, had not worked outside of the home but still struggled with empty nesting, grand-parenting, the loss of their parents, eggshell walking with married children, and those condescending "yes dears and sweeties" that often marginalize us in later life.

The difference between us was that most of these non-career women had burrowed themselves into longtime passions and newly created interests. It seemed that between raising their children, caring for homes, and managing lives, they had carved out space for self-fulfillment. One of my friends spent mornings in her garden. She dug, planted, and watered perennials, sunflowers, and poppies. She shared photos of wicker baskets brimming with red and yellow flowers scattered throughout her home. Another devoted much of her day to meditating, stretching, weightlifting, and sweating on her exercise bike. In the late afternoons she replenished her sweat with smoothies and a shower, and blow dried her hair. A third relished cooking and entertaining. She visited farmers' markets and specialty grocers shopping for wild salmon, plump red tomatoes, and fresh avocado. She harvested recipes and hosted guests at theme-centric tables. There were also the sporting women who played-tennis or golf and those who played games like mahjong, bridge, and pickle ball. Many were active in organizations and were longtime members of Hadassah, sisterhoods, and giving circles. Some even found joy in cleaning. "I took down all my screens, hosed them off, and Windexed the windows," a friend exclaimed to me on the telephone. I said, "sounds great!" but thought *you gotta be kidding.*

Then there were the women like the one I met in the nail salon. They were grateful to be finished with schedules, bosses, and stress. They worked and saved their entire lives for the freedom to travel, explore, read, watch TV, or simply rock in their favorite chair. They saw retirement as a well-earned gift.

I didn't judge any of these women. I was jealous of them.

Was the void larger for those of us driven with unbridled ambition, who thrived on pressure, or like me, had something to prove? Those of us whose work was our calling, our identity, our addiction—a fix, an adrenaline high.

I sought out women with careers that were similar to mine. I learned that our generation (baby boomers) were charting new ground in dealing with retirement issues. We were the first to climb the professional ladders in numbers, and now we were working our way down without role models to keep us from crashing. Clinging to the banister of hope for new purpose.

I also learned that many retired career women re-entered the workforce, took on full-time non-profit roles, or became consultants. They preferred to maintain their professional personae rather than reframe priorities and identities.

To avoid putting anyone on the defensive, I asked, "How do you spend your time?" rather than, "What do you do?" Most said, "I'm busy. I'm terribly busy."

I wondered why, like me, they revered full schedules. Maybe I wasn't the only one who sought to compensate for other perceived inadequacies. Was busy the new rich and thin? Was this just another way to avoid never feeling good enough?

I thought back to a colleague who had taken an early retirement to sail the Nile. At the time, I judged him. How dare he flee from productivity? He had abdicated corporate goals and accountability.

But perhaps he was on to something.

Why had I shied away from unstructured time as if it were carcinogenic?

I wanted my life to progress as more than a series of distractions from purposelessness, but I didn't know how to do it.

MY HANDS FLUTTERED in anticipation as I ripped open the large green envelope that showed up in my mail. It was an invitation to a law firm holiday party. Smiling to myself, I thought, *my name is still on an invitation list.*

When I was working and immersed in the legal and professional communities, I juggled party invitations like the many black pants that hung in my closet. Which ones did I have to attend? Who would be insulted if I didn't show up? Which one did I want to go to because I knew I'd have fun?

Now, the invitations had slowed to a halt. Until today.

Yet, before I had a chance to see if an RSVP was required, I had second thoughts. Did I still belong? I no longer had much in common with my former colleagues. I did not care what partner switched to which law firm or who was awarded a government contract. Yet I missed being part of the fray: the camaraderie of clients and friends, the inside humor, the pride of being an insider. I used to feel like the belle of the ball when I entered a room of lawyers. I'd stand near the bar, wine in hand, surrounded by cohorts who were curious about our business model, sometimes envious, over my transformation from practicing law to selling legal services. "How lucky are you?" a six-foot tall, gray-haired litigator commented one time.

"Why do you say that? With your reputation for winning, you're the one everyone envies," I shot back.

"But you never have to worry about billable hours—you get to concentrate on bottom line earnings instead."

I thought, *I am lucky.*

From the back of my closet, I pulled out a pair of black, wool, designer pants and a green, silk jacket to wear over a tank top. Then I was seized by a moment of panic. I no longer had business cards, those three-and-a-half-inch by two-inches rectangular pieces of paper that delineated my identity. What if someone at the party wanted to follow up, make plans for lunch? How would they reach me? If somebody handed me their card, wouldn't it be rude not to reciprocate? And *without a business card who was I?*

I thought about the first time that Mark and I ordered business cards. We struggled with the name of our company and our personal titles. When that first box was finally delivered to our office, I immediately broke through the tape and took out a handful of cards. I caressed the thick stock, running my thumb over my name, "Laura Black, CEO."

I didn't want to attend this party without something to hand out, so I ordered personal cards that had my name not followed by a job title or a company name. The off-white card also included my email address and telephone number printed in eighteen-point black font and surrounded by a red border.

In the past, I'd go to these parties on my own, sparing Charles from being sequestered in a corner listening to someone go on about their latest court win or lucrative settlement. Now, however, I needed the security of having him with me in case I felt out of place.

"Honey," I said as I showed him the invitation, "Will you come with me to this party?"

"You want me to?" he asked, surprised.

"Yeah. We don't have to stay long, just show our faces, then we can sneak out and go to dinner."

Six weeks later, we walked up to the registration desk of a downtown hotel, its ballroom transformed into a cabaret. I peeled the backing off of a name tag and stuck it to the right side of my jacket. I looked around the room and spotted some old friends. Between sips of wine, checking in with Charles, and circling the venue for quick chats with old connections, time passed. Yet, I knew, I was now as out of place in this room of movers and shakers as I had been at a recent dinner party with a group of women.

A friend had invited a handful of couples to her home for an impromptu dinner. As we mingled over drinks and appetizers, I overheard a group of men discussing asset allocations. I was intrigued, as I had recently thought about upping the fixed side of my portfolio. When I tried to break into the conversation, they ignored me. One of the women came over and said, "If you wouldn't mind, we could use an extra pair of hands in the kitchen to help clear away the hors d'oeuvres and make room for dinner."

Although I was never paid unfairly, I had fought hard for equality in the professional world. I remembered my second year of law school, when I spent the summer clerking for a firm and hoping to receive a full-time offer of employment at the end of the term. I was in the library doing research when one of the partners called me into his office. "Laura," he began, "something has come up and we need Bill to work on another matter. Would you mind researching the mechanic's lien issue that he was working on over the weekend?"

I said, "of course," thrilled for the chance to jump-in and impress him. My mood changed the following Monday morning when I ran into Bill and asked him, "So, how did it go? Did they assign you to an interesting case?"

Bill had no clue what I was talking about. He said, "They didn't give me any legal work, they needed me as a fourth for a golf tournament."

I never said anything to the partners. Whining would not help me achieve my career goals. But like my friend at the club having lunch with other female lawyers, I was keenly aware of the uphill battle to achieve parity.

After that incident, I worked hard to earn respect from my peers, both male and female. And with the success of the business, they began to take me seriously. Their respect grew in sync with our revenue.

Now that my status had changed, their interest waned.

Where did I belong?

It was not that I couldn't converse with these people at the party in the ballroom, it was that they represented the past and

I didn't know the future. At one time I saw leaders in the legal and corporate ranks as current or potential clients. I wanted to connect with them and either earn or keep their business. Now, I felt like a has-been, a nobody.

After a couple of hours, I found Charles, grabbed his hand, walked past a large man blowing a brass trombone, and we left.

16

A Boca Bubbie

"HI, BEA," SAID Marco, the valet, with a smile. "Happy Thanksgiving. You look extra beautiful tonight. Just give me a second and I'll help you."

Mom was wearing fall colors for the holiday, a rust and green print jacket with matching accessories and a bright orange lipstick. She had gone to the beauty salon earlier that afternoon, and when Marco retrieved her walker from the trunk of Dad's car, she had shot him a look that said, "Aren't you going to say how nice I look?"

Slipping Marco a twenty dollar bill, Dad said, "Thank you and Happy Thanksgiving to you and your family. I hope you'll have a chance to get some turkey and pumpkin pie tonight."

It was the Wednesday before the holiday, and after numerous summit-level discussions, my siblings and I had capitulated to dinner at the Club, our family shorthand for clubhouse. My parents dined there three to four nights a week. It was their safe place, a part of our family tapestry. The Club was the hub of a sprawling, South Floridian, green-grassed community of condominiums, golf courses, tennis courts, boat slips, walking paths, and a gym. My parents had lived there for thirty years. My father's picture hung in the foyer of the clubhouse, along with those of other past HOA presidents. At one time I felt pride that he was elected to this position and later, gratitude that it fed his self-esteem. My mother navigated to the handicapped-friendly bathroom, and I felt slightly guilty for not going with her.

The maître d' escorted my parents to "their" table, located in the back-left corner of the floral-carpeted, wood-paneled dining room. I held my breath as my father wobbled across the room, anchoring himself by grabbing onto chairs and tables along the way. I pleaded, "Dad, please use a cane. This is silly. If you fall and break your hip..."

He said, "I'm fine. I'm fine. I have one in the car."

Charles focused on my mother. He pulled out her cushioned armchair and strategized about where to leave her walker.

"Leave it where I can reach it," she ordered.

I inhaled the sweet aroma of gardenias and roses, thankful that the club catered to a diversity of ages, and there wasn't a musty smell.

When my parents spotted friends they exchanged head nods and visited their tables. They bragged, "The kids flew in from Baltimore to have Thanksgiving with us." This was their code for, *"Our kids love us so much that they traveled from all the way up north to be with us for the holidays."*

I exchanged niceties with their friends while keeping a look-out for a waiter. One of the long-time servers caught my eye and raced to bring my parents their iced teas before taking our drink orders. My father opened a pink Sweet and Low packet for my mother, trying not to call undue attention to her arthritic fingers.

After perusing the menu in hope of a new daily special, I settled down and focused on my parents in the same way that I used to assess Jackie to determine whether she was dressed too provocatively for a school dance. I took in my father's stooped posture and sallow complexion as well as my mother's thinness, fragile frame, and shaking hand. It had only been six weeks since I last visited but each time I saw them, a little more of them had disappeared. Dad was eighty-four and Mom was eighty-two.

A new, crushing awareness flattened me—they were failing. Whether it was weeks, months, or even a few years, their time was measured. And it was never going to be long enough.

The distance between wondering and knowing is vast, and the former leaves space for denial. I could not, did not, want to picture a world without my parents; that was too painful, flattening, and disorienting on a primal level. I moved away from these thoughts as if they were dangling electrical wires, and focused on football, movies, and tomorrow's Thanksgiving dinner. I wanted now to last forever, a wish that was impossible to fulfill.

Despite my attempts at distraction, fear refused to relinquish its hold on me.

I needed to know:

"How does it feel when you can see the end?"

"What do you tell yourself to keep yourself going?"

"How much time do you spend thinking about the past?"

"Do you entertain dreams of immortality?"

"Do you experience joy or merely distractions from reality?"

My father interrupted my reverie with the question, "Who wants to share the bread pudding?"

Questions never asked are never answered.

After that dinner, with the same determination I had once used to score business deals and to guide college selections, I tried to optimize the final years of my parents' lives. I resolved to spend holidays, birthdays, and winters with them in Miami. I flew so often that I knew many of the airport ticketing agents and security personnel by name.

We ate dinners at their familiar neighborhood restaurants (I stopped advocating for new celebrity-chef venues). I devoured the daily special at the Club as if I were feasting on caviar in a Parisian bistro overlooking the Seine. I cracked stone crab claws from a tattered vinyl booth in a seafood restaurant that sat on a busy highway and pretended I was in South Beach at Joe's. And

I ate Pad Thai from an Asian restaurant in a busy strip mall and said, "This is as good as the old Mr. K's in New York." I quit urging them to travel and gave up on the idea of a family cruise. I accepted my mother's obsession with slot machines and my father's escapism through poker. And, in the same manner I once placed my hand over the heart of my babies to confirm that they were breathing, I called them multiple times a day "just to check in."

I jumped into a chance for accountability to ace this final test, to measure up as the consummate daughter.

MY PARENTS' DECLINING health magnified awareness of my own aging. I began noticing changes in my own household, like the transition of the contents of my medicine cabinet from children's Tylenol, Bacitracin, and Band-Aids to Visine, Preparation-H, and Tums.

Simple acts, like when I got dressed for a meeting with a pair of thirty-something women at one of those nouveau coffeehouses, threw me into a tizzy. I felt safe encased in the armor of my go-to uniforms for board meetings and lunches with contemporaries at business clubs, but these executives were the same age as my kids.

My wardrobe was centered around forty pairs of black pants (thirty-seven of them had elastic waists, the other three I never wore). Not that I needed to justify, but I required different lengths, fabric weights, and (especially) sizes. They ran the gamut from tight-fitting to wide legged, or what we used to call bell bottoms.

I stood in front of my full-length mirror and tried on several black pants and top/jacket combinations. Finally, I settled on a pair of medium-weight pants and a navy hip-length top. I hoped I looked somewhat stylish. I was tempted to ask Alexa, "Does this make me look old?" If she answered, "No," I would add, "Does it make me look fat?"

In the last few years, like many parts of my body, my confidence in fashion had sagged. My angst was not limited to business meetings with millennials. Simply packing for vacation was cause for confusion. I wondered: Was it okay to wear a fanny pack? How about my extra-wide and super-thick New Balance tennis shoes? (Those dainty white sneakers don't have enough arch support.) And, if it's hot, could I wear sleeveless tops, even if my underarms jiggled? How about shorts? Was I past the "appropriate" age limit? Were capris better? Would they make me look like a Boca Bubbie?

Black-tie events brought a deluge of decisions. Was pantyhose still fashionable? If so, nude or black? Heels were out for me, and wedges didn't work either; after a few drinks, they made me wobble. I needed flat and fashionable footwear, but wide enough to accommodate custom orthotics. Would I be condemned if I showed up in SAS rather than Manolo Blahnik?

Like technology, I'd kept up enough to get by but I always ran into problems. The difference was, when my computer froze, my husband could help. But where would I turn to find out if eyeliner was in? And, if it was, did it go on both the top and bottom of my lids? Getting more personal, was *everything* supposed to get waxed?

And those undergarments that I think are called shapers. Admittedly, they're much better than the old girdles and long-line bras. But while they sucked in my stomach and hips, somehow, like ants in the summer, my fat found a way to escape. I tried thongs from Victoria's Secret. I wore a purple pair for a few hours but I just didn't get the appeal. I knew my granny panties weren't a turn-on but my tush was grateful.

Looking for fashion direction, I observed other women in my age group. Some fought like David against the Goliath of aging. They subjected their bodies to lifts, tucks, and fillers. They wore jeans with holes and boots without toes. And many of them carried it off. I didn't.

On the other extreme were the women who surrendered to age without fighting. They wore floral house dresses or fashion favorites from the seventies. They didn't have to lug plastic bags of clothes to Goodwill. For them, nothing was out of style.

The group I most admired had a knack for classic dressing. Their silver hair and designer scarves epitomized elegance. They didn't concern themselves with what was in—they reached for what was timeless. They walked tall and confident and embraced their maturity. I couldn't tie a scarf.

I could make an appointment with a fashion consultant. Or I could study *Vogue* and shop at Saks. But, whenever I learned the rules, the game changed, and nobody sent me an alert. More importantly, I didn't care enough to stay up-to-date. As my granddaughter said when we were shopping for a dress for her graduation, "I want to be myself, but I don't want to stick out so much that other people talk."

When I got to the coffee shop, one of the millennials wore a dress with a denim jacket, the other wore jeans and a black top. Between sips of java and bites of avocado toast, they expressed interest in my writings.

On the way out, the one in the denim jacket said, "You look great for your age." In other words, it didn't matter what I wore because, in their eyes, I was old. I hoped they also noticed that I was full of life, vitality, and wisdom.

17

Giving Up and Giving In

HOPING THAT NO one else was watching, I climbed upon the seat of an adult tricycle and pedaled. I hated it. It was heavy and unwieldy—not an acceptable replacement for my two-wheeled Schwinn. I loved that bicycle with its fat tires, cushy seat, and clunky wire basket that held my water bottle, lock, and purse. But I'd been afraid to ride it since my fall the summer before.

Charles and I had been riding our bikes to breakfast. When we approached the restaurant, he took a sharp right turn, over the curb and into the parking lot. I tried to follow. But the next thing I knew, I was splayed on the ground as awkward as an offensive lineman in a tutu.

Passersby offered help but I declined with embarrassment. Charles lifted the bike off my chest, and we assessed the damage: bruises and blood, but nothing gushy or worthy of stitches (although later, my left knee swelled, seemingly with humiliation, and I had to have it drained).

Charles helped me to my feet and after asking, "You, okay?" He said, "Honey, your bike was parallel to the curb, that's why you fell. You should have turned the wheel and crossed it at a right angle." I thought, "How was I supposed to know that?" And in that moment, my confidence as a cyclist collapsed. I walked the bike home and buried it in the back of our storage closet. I hadn't touched it for over a year, and I missed it.

Unless I counted walking, riding a bike was my only outdoor activity (I never mastered tennis, diving, hiking, surfing, or skiing, to name a few alternatives). At the beach, I would ride up and down the Coastal Highway, exploring bayside and oceanfront communities. I'd cycle south to the Boardwalk and north to downtown Bethany. On a trip to Wyoming, Charles, my daughter, and I pulled over for a herd of buffalo when we biked on mountain trails. In Vancouver, I biked with my sister and our daughters around the Seawall Trail in Stanley Park. And one of my most memorable trips was biking with my brother and sister-in-law in Monterey.

Biking had allowed me to see myself as active. But after the fall I was afraid to ride as well as afraid not to. A tricycle, with its two back wheels for balance, was a last-ditch attempt to resurrect my self-image.

The Eastern Shore bike shop was jam-packed with merchandise. I had combed through mazes of racing bikes, mountain bikes, road bikes and even bicycles built for two. But I couldn't find what I was looking for. Before long, a pony-tailed salesman with tattoo-covered biceps greeted me and asked, "Can I help you?"

And, in the same voice I used the first time I asked a male drugstore clerk for a box of tampons, I muttered, "Do you have any adult tricycles?"

To his credit, he didn't laugh, "Give me a minute, I think there's one in the back." Before I had time to change my mind, he came out with that red three-wheeler. It looked like an adult-sized version of the ones I bought my kids when they were toddlers, minus those multi-colored plastic strips hanging off the handlebars.

"Let's take it out to the parking lot so you can give it a try."

I wanted to love it, but I didn't even like it.

The problem was bigger than bicycling. Like another wrinkle between my brows, anxiety had marred my self-assurance. I vacillated before driving my rental car on I-95 from Miami to Delray Beach. I hung my trifocals from my blouse before stepping on steep escalators. And I went out of my way to avoid walking on ice and snow.

I conceded apprehension but feared capitulation. Wasn't giving up the same as giving in? I had not wanted to succumb to self-imposed limitations. I had little control over the insidious losses that come with aging, but I could control how I handled them. I could choose fight over flight.

When I returned from the tricycle fiasco, I dragged my two-wheeler out of the storage closet, pumped air into its tires, and tossed my stuff into the basket. Grabbing the black rubber handlebars, I maneuvered it into the elevator and out to the street. Then I buckled the strap of my helmet under my chin and straddled the seat. Inhaling courage and exhaling fear, I pedaled north on the Coastal Highway. I was free. It was just like riding a bike. Once you learn, you never forget.

BREATHLESSLY, A FRIEND called and said, "Laura, did you hear, Margi had a heart attack?"

"Oh, my God! No!"

"Listen, it's ok. She's ok. She's in the hospital. She's having surgery tomorrow and she should be home by Sunday."

Margi survived the surgery. When we spoke the next day, in typical Margi fashion, she made sure I understood the warning signs of a heart attack. But then the unthinkable happened. While still in the hospital, her blood pressure plummeted, and she died. No one could save her.

I first met Margi and her husband in the early 1980s when my family moved into the small, mock Colonial-style house next door. The movers were still unloading boxes when our doorbell rang. I opened the door to a pair of matching, full-faced smiles, a warm banana bread, and a heartfelt greeting, "Welcome to the neighborhood."

Had we not moved in next door, Margi and I would never have been friends. She was Mary Richards while I was Rhoda Morgenstern from that iconic Mary Tyler Moore Show. She loved wearing brightly-colored blouses and scarved tied perfectly. I wore jeans and black shirts, and I hated scarves. Margi was focused and deliberate while I was impulsive and messy. She wore her deep brown (later grey) hair in a short, no-fuss style. I spent hours with blow dryers and straighteners. She devoured "Hints from Heloise," and I preferred "Valley of the Dolls."

Fortunately, our physical proximity allowed me to see the Margi behind those scarves. Sipping morning coffees and evening wines, I learned to treasure her prophetic wisdom, "In life you get a limited number of nickels—I want to spend mine with people that I care about." I respected her commitment to helping the vulnerable: she volunteered at a center for displaced women, taught Sunday school, and personally delivered food to the homeless. Over time, I grew to not only admire her, but to love her.

During the weeks and months after her death I did my best to adjust to the loss of my friend. Slowly, my wound began to scab. However, a new and deeper one, developed: Margi wasn't that much older than me.

I grew even more sensitive to the signs of aging. I winced when Medicare fliers appeared in my mailbox. I felt the aching in my knees and the throbbing in my fingers. I hated the AARP card even though I used it.

I was a teenager when I lost my maternal grandmother and a young adult when my other grandparents died. While I was overwhelmed by the concept of permanent absence, their losses did not bleed into borders that touched my own mortality.

I missed my friend and longed for her wisdom, insight, and loyalty. I flashed back to the picture that hung on Margi's living room wall. She and her family were poised, in coordinating khakis and whites, on a sand dune in Rehoboth Beach. Now she was gone, just like that.

THE MEDICAL CENTER bustled with weary-faced patients dressed in baggy bottoms and untucked shirttails. Their designated drivers waited in stiff armchairs, reading Kindles, working on laptops, or playing games on iPads. When Charles checked in, the receptionist eyed my brown cardboard to-go cup of coffee and said, "I'm sorry, you have to throw that away." Pointing to a sign, she continued, "See, it says, 'No Food or Drink.' It is not fair to the patients. There could be a mob riot." I gulped down the remainder of my coffee in the hallway.

Of all my marital responsibilities, taking my husband for a colonoscopy was at the bottom of the list. This man, who lifted two hundred-pound barbells and said root canals were "no big deal" worked himself into a tither at the thought of forced fasting and cleansing. So, I steadied myself for the fallout when he said, "I scheduled a colonoscopy next month. I need you to take me."

"Is everything okay?"

"Yeah, it's just routine."

My next thought, which I kept to myself, was, *If it's just routine, why didn't you check with me first, to see what worked with my schedule?*

Two weeks before the "big day," Amazon delivered a case of extra-strength toilet paper. Later that week, I opened the refrigerator and counted eighteen bottles of apple juice, a case of lemon vitamin water, a dozen lime Jell-O cups, four liters of ginger ale, and, in the freezer, an assortment of Italian ices. Shaking my head, I said, "I thought you were only on liquids for a day?"

He said, "Yes, one *whole* day." Then he added, "Do you think scotch counts as a clear liquid?"

For the rest of the week, Charles' conversation focused on where he should eat his "last meal." I rolled my eyes when I replied, "Wherever you want." We ended up at an Italian restaurant where he ate as if he was preparing for six months of hibernation. On the way home, he swapped obsessions and wondered where should he eat breakfast after the procedure?

The night of his prep, to escape from the cacophony of moans, groans, and flushing toilets, I went out to dinner with a girl-friend. I came home to a barrage of questions: "What did you eat? Describe it in detail; I need vicarious satisfaction. Do you have any idea how hungry I am?"

The following morning, as soon as he could break free from the bathroom, I drove him to the out-patient center for his 9 a.m. appointment. He insisted on arriving by 8:30 a.m. "just to be safe."

I tossed my coffee cup in the trash, settled in next to Charles, and waited for them to call him back. A steady stream of patients waddled from the waiting room to the bathroom. I too, needed a restroom, but there was no way I was going to use that one.

At 10 a.m. we were still waiting. I was hungry. Before we left home, I had stuffed a pack of peanut butter crackers into my purse. Like a spy, I reached in my handbag and, one at a time, cupped a cracker into my palm, shoved it in my mouth, and chewed it without moving my jaw.

At 10:30 a.m. a statuesque nurse with a clip board shouted, "Mr. Charles!"

I asked, "Can I go back with him?"

"No. Leave us your phone number and come back in an hour and a half."

I went across the street to a nail salon for a gel manicure and to use their restroom. The receptionist had said to be back by noon. I was back by 11:30 a.m. I busied myself with my iPhone, glancing at the door every five seconds, hoping to see Charles walk out.

Thirty minutes later, concern replaced annoyance. Charles had gone back for his colonoscopy at 10:30 a.m. and they said he'd be finished by noon. It was now 12:45 p.m. Since Margi's passing, I scared easily when it came to health. I couldn't help but worry, *what if something had gone wrong: a suspicious growth, too much anesthesia, an allergic reaction?* Like a kite caught up in gale-force winds, my angst took off, and with it, guilt.

I had laughed at Charles' preparations and his own anxiety and felt put out that I had to escort him to his appointment. I should have been grateful that he took care of himself. Colonoscopies save lives. True, he had been a tad obsessive and hangry, but that hardly tipped the scales.

Please don't let anything be wrong.

Just as I was pleading with the receptionist to check on him, the door swung open and out walked Charles. He was holding films.

"Is everything okay?"

"Yeah, fine."

"Are you sure?"

"Yes, do you want to see the pictures of my colon?"

"No, thank you."

I held his hand as we walked outside and got into the car. Then I smiled and said, "Where would you like to go for breakfast?"

18

Woo-Woos

MY PARENTS WERE declining, my dear friend passed away, and for the first time I had envisioned losing Charles. My sense of time shifted. The future held less than the past. I tried to stay in the moment and practice gratitude. I took meditation classes but could not meditate longer than two minutes. I downloaded apps that instructed me to count my breaths. When I remembered to, I'd list ten things I was grateful for before going to sleep each night.

Nevertheless, as the ticking of passing moments grew louder, I fought to silence the voice inside me that said, "You must be more productive. Take control and call the shots."

I thought back to all the times that I had negotiated business deals. I demanded, I was confident, and I had power. Now, time was racing away from me and I was frozen, desperate for goals and markers. If I couldn't measure where I was going, how would I know when I had arrived? What was I striving for? Was there a reason to strive?

I'd always been accountable. At first, it was wrapped up in education, in grades and class rank. Later, in my career, in profit margins and sustainability. I measured myself as a mother, a wife, and as a sister.

Must there always be a goal? Did I need to fabricate some, like visiting all of the states, reading the Great Books, or becoming a master at bridge? What if I didn't care about any of these things? How could I grant myself permission to relax and let my life unfold, to switch seats from driver to passenger, so to speak?

These thoughts were swirling around in my head when I ran into an old friend at the café in Nordstrom's. After we caught each other up on our families, she said, "I received an unexpected inheritance from my aunt."

"That's great!" I said.

"I'm not sure what to do with the money."

"That should be your worst problem! But, seriously, what are you thinking?"

"I will probably just save it; but it would be nice to..."

"To what?"

"I don't know, do something different."

"Like what?"

"I'm not sure—nothing too crazy, nothing too woo-woo."

I asked, "What is wrong with woo-woo?"

I wondered, *what is wrong with replacing some of that productivity with fun and frivolity?*

I used to have woo-woos. I went to the circus and licked fingers sticky with pink cotton candy. I had pancakes for dinner and pizza for breakfast. I climbed on the hood of my father's car and gazed at the stars in pajamas. I wore white organza dresses embroidered with red roses that my grandmothers made by hand.

Later, woo-woos were tinged with naughtiness. I hitch-hiked with a girlfriend in college, smoked in the back seat of a car, and downed one too many sugar-laced alcoholic concoctions.

With career and family, responsibility, and exhaustion, woo woos had vanished. With more tasks than hours, I stopped even considering taking time for frivolity. Had I turned into a bit of a martyr? Did part of me flourish in sacrifice? Had I allowed myself to become a victim?

My friend at Nordstrom's had recoiled from the concept of woo-woos as if it were an infected man's sneeze. I now realized that I was guilty of the same. My most daring act in the last few years had been getting back on my bike; the naughtiest act was taking a scoop of ice cream on top of my apple pie.

Why did everything have to be purposeful and productive? Could I give myself permission to binge on a TV series during the day? Maybe curl up on a rocker and sink into a romance book? How about some karaoke with friends? Perhaps it was time to be spontaneous and to live in the moment. Enough with always analyzing, calculating. Not every activity needed a direction, a plan. It was time to "go with the flow."

The following week at the beach, a friend called me and said, "It's such a beautiful day. How about you and Charles coming out with me and Mike on our boat?" Our kitchen island was covered with reports that I had brought with me to review for an upcoming non-profit board meeting. Looking at the paperwork, I was about to say, "No thank you," but remembering my promise said, "Sure, we'd love it!" For the first time in years, I put on a bathing suit.

As the boat sped through the waters of Assawoman Bay, the wind blew my hair and I put a strap around my neck to keep my glasses from falling off. The condominium buildings on the shore receded, and my attention shifted to the seagulls flying overhead and to the mesmerizing movement of the sea. Mike slowed to a half throttle when we spotted a cluster of wild ponies galloping through the marshes of Assateague Island. A chocolate-colored mare stood apart from the others, lovingly nuzzling her foal. How natural this maternal love, so beautiful and affirming.

How many experiences like this had I missed in my stubborn insistence on productivity?

19

Downsizing

CLINGING TO THE banister with a death-like grip, I turned sideways to minimize the pressure on my knees, and step by step made my way downstairs for breakfast. At the pinewood kitchen table, accompanied by seven empty, tan, Naugahyde chairs, I drank coffee from a mug decorated with my former business logo. Charles had left for work and the kids now lived in houses or apartments of their own.

Charles and I only used three rooms of our six-bedroom, three-level contemporary home: the bedroom, the kitchen, and the den. There was no longer a reason to venture down to the basement, where the billiards table monopolized the main room and where Andy's bedroom had been, long abandoned. I hadn't yet cleaned out Andy's bureau, and I didn't have the wherewithal to tackle the drawers that overflowed with t-shirts embossed with little league team names, odd socks, and underwear faded yellow with time. I dreaded entering the L-shaped storage closet which contained twenty-five years' worth of stuff that we held onto "just in case," like wheelless old luggage, poster board collages, and a full set of *World Book Encyclopedias.*

Our over-sized, kidney-shaped pool took up the back yard and required a degree in chemistry to concoct the magic formula that would keep the water clear. Additionally, insects, frogs, and leaves had claimed its frigid water for their home. I'd given up trying to scoop them out with a long-handled net.

The house had provided a serene oasis away from my day-to-day work life. Now that I had nothing to escape from, it was lonely and isolating. I yearned for connection as I took quiet walks on tree-lined streets. I wanted hustle and bustle rather than the songs of crickets and smells of fresh-mowed grass. I ached for a neighborhood coffee shop where the barista knew my name and pulled up a chair to talk with me while I sipped on a cappuccino at *my* table. Maybe a bookstore. When I'd come in to browse a staffer would say, "The new Anne Tyler book was delivered today."

It was time to downsize, but that was another loss. I hated change. It took us almost five years to make the transition, but eventually we sold the house that I worked so hard not to sell and moved into a condominium on Baltimore's Inner Harbor, near boats, coffee shops, bookstores, and the bustle of people.

The adjustment was easier than I had imagined it would be. On our first night in the freshly painted apartment, our next-door neighbors came over to welcome us. They were generous with offers to help us unpack and had easy laughs and quizzical minds. As an added perk, they had a spunky five-year-old daughter who brought us a freshly plucked "welcome to the neighborhood" daisy.

The move gave me temporary purpose, a distraction. I flipped through house magazines and searched websites for the look I wanted (this was my chance to create a decor from scratch). I was drawn to a mixture of styles, such as modern sofas and tables accented with antiques. I interviewed decorators and hired a woman who "got" my vision. We customized closets and hung TVs.

I unpacked a large brown cardboard box stuffed with markings of my professional career. There were eight-by-ten-inch framed *"Maryland's Top 100 Women"* awards, *"Wise Woman"* plaques, *"Entrepreneur of the Year"* scrolls, college and law school diplomas, and trophies for leadership. Decades of tangible manifestations of my accomplishments. But I didn't need them anymore, there was no one to impress. One by one I put them back in their box and asked Charles to carry it downstairs to the storage locker.

I became part of a new group of eclectic and diverse neighbors who, like me, craved the clatter of city life. Twice a day, Charles or I would walk Einstein, our Cavachon, around the perimeter of the harbor where we'd meet other dogs and their owners. Before long, Charles knew everybody (and their pets) by name. Oftentimes, I'd stop to rest on one of the metal benches that lined the water and I'd gaze out to the bay as sailboats, kayaks, water taxis, and motorboats sailed by. I was filled with gratitude for this new lifestyle and did my best to ignore the feeling in the pit of my stomach that I still needed more, but what?

20

Mother-in-Law Marginalization

I THOUGHT BACK to the time, over forty years ago, when in his off-key voice my father sang, "Hate to see you go. Hate to see you go. Hope the heck you never come back. Hate to see you go." My grandmother laughed so hard that she snorted. We were driving her to the airport to fly back to her apartment in New York after visiting us in Miami.

With good humor, she put up with all the mother-in-law teasing. "Do you know why fathers-in-law die before mothers-in-law?" he'd prod.

"Why?" she'd ask, taking his bait.

"Because they want to," he replied, thinking that he was funnier than Rodney Dangerfield

And now I was a mother-in-law. It felt like another loss of status.

Danny, my eldest son, had married Laura, a sensitive and beautiful photographer who looked at life through a wide lens and had more patience than a psychotherapist. Seven years later, Andy married Kristin, a stunning artist with an engaging personality who was comfortable coming to breakfast in her pajamas the first time she slept at our house.

Once again, I was bereft of reliable role models to guide me through the process of being a mother-in-law. My mother had been polite, indulgent, and respectful to her own mother-in-law, but I had no memories of tight hugs or long telephone calls from either party.

My father, with his condescending songs and jokes, had been no better.

I did not want to be painted with that brush. I was determined to be different.

I considered the irony that I had climbed elusive ladders, struggled with high-stress careers, managed a family, advocated for social justice, insisted on equality, demanded respect, and refused to take a back seat to anyone, unless, of course, it was my daughters-in-law, because I was afraid of them.

When my sons slid those rings (the ones I helped select and pay for) on their beloveds' fingers, power seeped through the gold. And that power had potential to punish.

One of my girlfriends confided to me, "My daughter-in-law asked me to watch the kids next Friday. I told her I couldn't because I had a doctor appointment."

"What's wrong with that?"

"It was a lie. I didn't want to admit I was going to yoga."

I understood. She feared her daughter-in-law's wrath. With the flick of a hormone, her daughter-in-law could veto a family dinner, renege on Sunday brunch, or withhold the grandchildren.

There are no movements or rallies, to my knowledge, addressing mother-in-law empowerment.

My generation chiseled away at obstacles so that the next one would have choices. Choices brought stress. I wanted to help these women find clarity, to prioritize, process, and juggle, if they'd let me in. I wasn't competing with them for first place with their husbands, my sons. They'd already won. I just wanted involved spectator status.

Once my boys were married, an innocuous question like "Do you want to have dinner Tuesday night?" required the consent of two parties, my sons *and* their wives. All the while I was left in a holding pattern, waiting for my request to reach the top of their to-do lists. Holidays became a negotiation more complicated than passing a bi-partisan bill in Congress. The kids were torn between their father (my ex-husband) and his extended family, their new wives and their families, and me and Charles.

It felt like I needed them more than they needed me, and I loathed being put into that position.

Tired of trying so hard, I tucked away my insecurities and ceased rushing the relationships with my daughters-in-law. A marriage license alone would not bridge the gap from losing a son to gaining a daughter.

I began to telephone my daughters-in-law for the where, when, and whys of proposed plans. As we got to know one another, we shared our vulnerabilities, much like I had done with former clients. Only now the stakes were much higher. I could have withstood not connecting with a customer, but not with the wives of my sons.

Our mutual respect grew as authenticity seeped through the wires. I stopped tiptoeing on those metaphorical eggshells. I'd had enough of swallowing my thoughts and blending into the background. I allowed myself to leak through the façade, as did they.

Soon, Laura began calling *me* to discuss summer plans, and Kristin called to share her latest remodeling project. Now we call each other regularly just to check in and say "hi."

I had been wrong to foolishly buy into that mother-in-law stigma. Over time I learned that I am more with them in my life, not less.

And I cherish our tight hugs and long phone calls.

21

Not a Greeting Card Grandma

I GRABBED MY cherub-faced granddaughter from my daughter-in-law's arms, kissed her forehead, tickled her tummy, and held her tight to my chest. It was Wednesday, my day to babysit. I spent the day cradling her in my arms while I wiggled the nipple of a bottle into her pink bud of her mouth. I changed diapers, adding an extra layer of Desitin, just to be sure. I made stupid faces and talked in silly voices hoping for a coo or a smile.

I also watched the clock.

Time crawled by. To help pass the long afternoons, I joined one of those "Mommy and Me" kind of classes. I held hands with the twenty-something Moms who wore work-out bras and leggings. We formed a circle and sang, "*Ring around the rosie...*" but I remained standing when we got to the "*all fall down.*"

I lasted for a year and then offered to pay for childcare.

Many of my friends filled their days by taking care of grandchildren when their own children went back to work. I had attempted to do the same. I would have cherished being with Addie every day, for an hour or two. But I did not want the full day, weekly responsibility.

And while Charles and I were happy to babysit with notice or crisis, we did not want to give up our weekend nights on a regular basis.

Was something wrong with me?

These thoughts brought up the residual guilt from raising my own children. But this time I stepped away and looked at it with aged eyes.

I thought back to when I was a new mother recovering from a C-section. In the quiet of 2 a.m. feedings, I'd rock my baby in a white wicker chair as tears of gratitude dripped down my cheek and landed on his.

During daylight hours, while he slept cocooned in a blanket, I'd straighten up the house. Unloading and reloading the dishwasher, again and again, I would cry, but this time because I was miserable. I craved conversation and challenge. I couldn't wait to return to work, which I did within a month of all three of births.

Why would I be different as a grandmother?

I had never been a homebody. I fled from domesticity. Aside from reading and writing, I had a hard time staying home and staying still. I'd sit on the floor for a game of Monopoly as long as we played the short version. I molded Play-Doh into tigers and lions but would rather have gone with my children to the zoo.

Addie, with her dark curly hair and never-ending curiosity was my first grandchild. Three years later she became a big sister to Connor and Zachary, identical twins. These grandchildren plugged the holes of our childless home and filled that deafening silence. When they visited, the house pulsed with energy and possibility. They sensed potential in the mundane. A pillow was a landing pad for a full-body cannonball. Paper clips were strung together for necklaces. There was no self-consciousness, no measured words, ulterior motives, no cunning manipulations. There was complete abandonment to the moment.

When Addie turned ten years old, Charles and I took her on a cruise to Alaska, during which we went whale watching. She explained to me that orcas are not whales but dolphins. We brought the boys to see the jaguar at the zoo in Miami. Often, I take the three of them to the beach where we lay on a blanket, look up to the stars, and share dreams.

It wasn't about selfishness. There is nothing I wouldn't do for my family. Self-absorption? No. I could get out of myself and see my children and grandchildren. I was always taking the pulse of their happiness. I wanted to know as much as they'd tell me about their lives and how they were coping. They knew that they could count on me and that I'd never let them down.

I needed to stop admonishing myself for living my truth. It came down to acceptance. I was not a stereotypical grandma. I was Bubbie—and that was good enough.

"COME TO STICKY'S and Gummy's funeral. It's in my room at 7:30. Wear black."

Sticky and Gummy were the five-cent, slimy, crystalline toys that Addie "won" at an amusement arcade the previous evening. (Given the amount of money we spent, I could have flown to Vietnam and bought them directly from the manufacturer.) The figurines met their demise when one of my grandsons stretched them to the point of dismemberment. Addie screamed, "Why did you do that?" Her brother apologized, "I was just playing. I didn't think they'd break." She accepted his apology but insisted on a proper funeral.

It was a humid late August day. Charles, my son's in-laws, and I had brought five children to the beach who ranged in age from four to ten. It was on day two of the trip when we adults sipped our first cups of morning coffee and the kids pleaded "more Pop Tarts" that Addie shooed us into her makeshift bedroom (a walk-in closet with a mattress) and all nine of us scrunched together to pay our last respects. Charles delivered the eulogy.

"Dearly beloved, we are gathered here today to celebrate the short lives of Sticky and Gummy..."

I tried to keep a solemn countenance but couldn't. The in-laws caught my eye and began to giggle. Soon, even the kids registered the absurdity of the situation, and we all broke into full-belly laughter. It was the first time since our arrival that I had let myself relax.

I couldn't help but flashback to my own childhood. What would it have felt like to be the center of the universe, to have my parents and grandparents focus their full attention on me and to receive that unconditional acceptance and awe over a triviality, like the planning of a funeral for a toy? Would that have prevented the void that ambition later filled but that was once again running dry and looking for replenishment?

I had to admit, bringing my grandchildren to the beach in my sixties was a far cry from taking my children there in my twenties. The walk from the condo to the water was longer. The softer, potholed sand was harder to navigate. The beach chairs and umbrellas were heavier. The sun was hotter and the noise was louder. I no longer enjoyed small hands wielding big shovels, burying any of my body parts in the sand. I didn't want to fill and refill buckets with water for castles that couldn't help but collapse. I just wanted to read my book.

I could deal with the commotion, heat, and exhaustion. It was the responsibility for their safety that put me over the edge. We spread our blanket in front of the lifeguard's feet. We forced the kids to wear Coast Guard-approved life jackets. We sprayed them every hour, from head to toe, with SPF 100 sunscreen. There were four adults watching five children. And still I was a nervous wreck.

I dragged my beach chair to the shallow waters. Sitting upright, I shaded my eyes with my hand, and tried to keep track of all of the children. Again and again, I counted out loud, "One, two, three, four, five. One, two, three, four, five..." I watched for the undertow that would sweep a child out to sea, the jellyfish with the poisonous sting, the fin of a Great White shark, or the kidnapper disguised as a fellow beachgoer.

Grandparent angst was not limited to vacations but began with Addie's birth. I quickly learned that, in addition to my own angst, I had to deal with a higher authority—her parents. I had to follow their rules (at least in their presence) and use pre-approved contraptions. Like the "one touch collapsible" stroller—it took months before I learned how to finagle it into my car trunk. And I never did figure out how to install the regulation car seat with all its straps and belts. In desperation, I paid a local firefighter to install it for me. I called him again when my daughter-in-law told me to change it from back-facing to front-facing. For years afterward, we took my husband's car if we were driving another couple to dinner so I wouldn't have to mess with the car seat.

My grandchildren were past the infant and toddler stages. This vacation was an opportunity to connect with them as people. Without their parents around, I didn't have to bother with limits on electronics, bedtimes, sugar intake, nor "use your words" jargon. Yet I had allowed hypothetical dangers to distract me from actual joys. Our laughter at the funeral for those cheap figurines slapped me into the moment. If I wanted more of those moments, I needed to ease up.

For the remaining couple of days, I allowed myself to be present. While we dealt with strep throat, pink eye, and sea lice, we also converted the kitchen island into a ping pong table and held tournaments. We built sand tunnels and collected seashells. We had a salami and egg cook-off and dessert at every meal.

After breakfast, on the last day of the trip, my grandson turned to me and said, "Bubbie, can we stay here forever?" I hugged him and answered, "Forever, no. But, hopefully next summer." It has become a yearly tradition. When we buried Sticky and Gummy, I buried my angst. Well, most of it.

PART IV

ROLE REVERSAL

22

No Hard Feelings

THE WAITER NODDED patiently as my mother instructed, "I'll have the salmon please. But make sure it's dry, no butter, no sauce, no spices."

He asked, "How about a little oil, salt or pepper?"

"No. Nothing. Plain."

Not long after we ordered, as we were eating, he returned and asked Mom, "How was the salmon?"

Without skipping a beat she said, "Dry with no taste."

Mom had become as helpless and pitiful as a goldfish going belly up in a tank. She had severe gastrointestinal issues and her Parkinson's was in full swing. She feared everything, from driving in the car with my father to eating most foods. Most of all she was terrified of losing my father. When he went out to play poker or run errands, she'd call him every thirty minutes "just to make sure he's okay."

Dad had heart issues and a wobbling gait. Their aging, once no more potent than a fleeting awareness, now filled me with dread and angst.

I put my own quest for purpose on pause to focus on my parents. I filed graduate program catalogues and "*How to Become a Personal Coach*" into the bottom drawer of the cabinet. I shelved my books about adjusting to retirement and purchased new ones on dealing with aging parents.

I welcomed the responsibility. It wasn't a sacrifice but a reprieve from my obsessive search for identity. My father had softened; he had turned into that kind of old that had a sweetness mixed into it. At a Mother's Day brunch with extended family members, he bought all of the women silver, beaded bracelets. He gave Addie, his great-granddaughter, pony rides on his knee. He ordered the king's cut of prime rib because he knew that I loved gnawing on the bone.

I would do my best to help them through this final phase of their lives. This became my new purpose and I embraced it whole-heartedly. Admittedly, part of my motives was self-serving. It was my way of saying to them, "no hard feelings."

MY FATHER'S INDEPENDENCE meant more to him than the hypothetical fall that worried us. He had become unsteady on his feet yet declined canes and walkers and insisted on caring for my mother on his own. He helped her into the shower, put on her shoes and socks, and wedged rubber inserts between her toes to keep them from rubbing together. We tried to convince him to hire an aide but he snapped, "Not while I'm around."

My sister and I despised bearing witness to the burden he carried. Perhaps it touched a nerve of guilt that we couldn't do more. Besides that, we were worried about him getting sick or having a heart attack. If something happened to my father, how would my mother manage? Wouldn't it make sense for them to move into a "caring community" together?

Gail and I looked into options and found a new, luxury, elder-care community not far from their home. While the sales manager sold us on the place, when we brought the brochure back to my father, he refused to even glance at the glossy sheets. On one page was the photograph of snappy, bald-headed men and spiffy, frail women clinking their glasses together in a toast. I could almost hear them shout, "L' Chaim" (to life). On another page, they were boarding a bus for an outing (I assumed to the opera or a play). On a third, they sat in velvet-cushioned armchairs in a chandeliered dining room chatting in earnest, perhaps about politics or estate planning.

We told Dad how the place had been designed by a famous architect and resembled a French villa. Valuable artwork hung from the walls and the aroma of fresh flowers filled common spaces. "And you remember the Bernsteins from the old neighborhood," I said, "we saw them in the lobby." I went on to point out the daily poker games for him and mahjong for my mother.

He wasn't impressed.

"I've heard enough," he said, with his *do not push me* voice. "If one of us gets hurt or dies the other one will have to figure it out. If Mom or I have to move later on, so be it. But for now, we love our home, and we are not making any changes."

I was frustrated but, at the same time, I understood. I wouldn't have wanted to move there or any other place that catered to the elderly. After my experience at fat girl's camp, I abhorred summer camps and organized group activities. Likewise, I never felt like I fit in with country club communities. When I reached my parents' age, I'd want to maintain my individuality and live near my kids. Granted, the place was magnificent and the activities abundant. The food was celebrity-chef worthy and the residents international and sophisticated. Yet even stronger than the scent of orchids that wafted through the halls was the pervasive aroma of loneliness—rotten, like old eggs.

Dad wanted to take care of Mom. She was the love of his life, and it gave him purpose. He did not ask for anything from me or my siblings. He had earned the right to choose how to live out his life. We would respect his wishes.

I rented an apartment in Coconut Grove, about a twenty-minute drive from their house. I stayed for the winters and visited them at least once a month during the rest of the year. I'd meet them for bagels at their deli and dinners at one of the three places where my mother was comfortable. I'd take Mom to the mall when she needed new pants or bras and my father to doctor appointments.

On one trip, I took him to a medical center for cataract surgery. On the drive home, Dad sat in the passenger seat wearing big, dark eyeglasses to protect his eyes from the light. He placed his hand on my shoulder and said, "Thank you."

I hated that he had to thank me and that my mother didn't have the wherewithal to take him for this simple procedure.

I said, "It's the least that I can do. Where should we go for lunch?"

ON THE EVENING of my father's eighty-fifth birthday party, he wore a new, blue suit and silver tie. He looked distinguished but pale. As the self-appointed master of ceremonies, he walked to the center of the room, took the microphone, and said, "There is nothing more important than family. You must always stay together and look out for one another. I love you. Now, let's celebrate!"

Dad had weathered a cardiac scare months after his cataract surgery, before this party. Mom called and said, "Daddy's having difficulty breathing. Dr. Newman wants to admit him to the hospital and run tests." I took the first flight out.

As he laid on the steel bed waiting for the test results, I tried to distract him by talking about anything except what we most feared: open heart surgery. In less time than I thought it would take, his doctor strolled into the room and said, "Your scans look ok; we thought you might need an aortic valve replacement but, for now, you're fine."

I was still digesting the doctor's words when my father sat up in his hospital bed and said to me, "Great. Now we can plan my eighty-fifth birthday party. Will you call the Club and make sure the party room is available?'

The party room at the Club was where we marked family milestones. Over the last three decades, my parents had hosted events from intimate dinners to lavish, white-glove affairs. When Andy graduated college, Dad hung a twelve-foot banner on the wall that read, in large, red letters, "Congratulations Graduate" and *cum laude* in a smaller font.

For my mother's sixty-fifth birthday, we rented a movie screen and played a video highlighting her life. For my father's seventieth, Mom sang Frank Sinatra's "My Way." At the time, Dad was in search of a renter for an investment property. My siblings and I, unable to find him a real tenant, gave him a box of ten ants (plastic ones). I can still see his lips curved into a smile, his body convulsing in laughter, as he processed the pun.

Of all our celebrations at the Club, my most cherished were holiday dinners. It was in that room that we broke Yom Kippur fasts and held Passover Seders. My mother made sure that the staff arranged tables into a large square so that no one felt excluded. The aroma of steaming sweet potato casseroles topped with charred marshmallows for Thanksgivings, matzah ball soup laced with dill for Passovers, permeated the room.

My mother would always steer the conversations back to herself, and my siblings and I would exchange eyerolls. After appetizers and salads, my father would tap his spoon against a crystal goblet, signaling for us to be quiet. Dad's speeches were consistent: he'd thank my mother, talk about the importance of family; mention gratitude; and in a booming voice and wide grin say, "It's time to eat!"

A couple of weeks after his hospitalization, he mailed invitations to close friends and family that read, "It's Time to Celebrate." He put a plastic watch inside each invitation.

Now we listened to his speech, grateful that he was able to celebrate his milestone birthday. We drank from an open bar, ate sushi and filet mignon from stations, and danced to the music of an aging trio.

I had no idea that three months later I'd walk into the Club for the very last time, to sit Shiva for my father.

AS A CHILD, I was jealous of Christmas.

Only one other Jewish family lived on our street in our South Florida neighborhood. While my family was still finishing leftover turkey sandwiches and soggy pumpkin pie, our neighbors were inflating plastic Santas and hanging colorful electric lights. I envied the stockings dangling from mock-fireplace mantles and the giant evergreens crowned with gold stars, their branches flaunting shiny red balls, like a bride-to-be showing off her engagement ring.

Our tiny wooden dreidels and shiny brass Menorah didn't stand a chance.

I sulked at this injustice until the year I turned ten, when my father took us on a bus tour of holiday lights. After our customary eggroll and egg foo young for Christmas Eve dinner, he drove my mother, seven-year-old brother, three-year-old sister, and me to the municipal building where we purchased our tickets and boarded the tour bus. Our driver, dressed as Santa, stood at the top of the steps and greeted us, one-by-one, with a deep, "Ho ho ho! Merry Christmas!"

The bus was crowded with families chattering in anticipation of singing elves and dancing snowmen. Little girls twirled in red velvet dresses and boys squirmed in plaid pants and green bow ties. I wore jeans and my favorite pink top. My brother and I argued over the window seat until Santa admonished, "sit down," as he pulled away from the curb. He drove us past the shops on Miracle Mile, rounded Alhambra Circle, and then pulled over at the first gawk-worthy house.

My nose was pressed against the window for a glimpse of the nativity scene when I heard a familiar, off-key voice singing "Rudolph the Red Nosed Reindeer."

"No way," I thought. "It couldn't be."

Mortified, I turned to the row behind me as my Jewish father went on, "had a very shiny nose." Blushing from my neck to my hairline, I yelled, "Dad, stop! What are you doing?" Then, after he chimed out, "and if you ever saw him," the other passengers joined in with, "you would even say it glows." Flashing me an ear-to-ear smile, he continued singing and led his choir from Rudolph to Frosty and other holiday favorites. Despite ourselves, it wasn't long before my siblings and I joined the chorus of "Jingle Bells." Before the two-hour tour was over, my father had the busload of passengers belting out "I Have a Little Dreidel."

Now, on Christmas Eve we still eat Chinese food, but instead of bus tours we go to the movies. During the Christmas of 2015, Charles and I went to a crowded theater to see the film about a woman who invented a special mop, starring Jennifer Lawrence. I was riveted by her tenaciousness and I was emotionally vested in her success. When the movie ended, Charles bolted outside for a cigar as I glanced at the credits and turned my cell phone back on. There were fifteen missed calls. My heart began racing and my hands shaking.

As the theater lights went on, I took a deep breath and I skimmed through the "recent calls" on my iPhone: my sister, my brother, my mother, my sister again, my brother again—all of them, again and again. Taking fast, shallow breaths, I browsed through my text messages: "Call me!" "Laura, you need to call me." "Wherever you are call me." "Call me."

I went outside, found Charles, and said, "Something's wrong. I think it's my father."

He steered me to a bench. A cold eeriness enveloped me, like my hand was slipping from the ledge of a mountain. I called my sister. She could hardly get out, "Hello."

"What's wrong?"

"Laura. Oh, my God. Laura. Are you sitting down?"

She cried even louder, and I strained to hear what I didn't want to know. Once I heard the words, I'd have to let go of hope.

"Tell me. Just tell me."

"Laura, Daddy died. He and mom were at the casino. He had a massive heart attack." Between raw sobs, she struggled to catch her breath.

"They called an ambulance to take him to Coral Gables Hospital. Harry and I met Mom there. They couldn't save him."

Now she was crying too hard to speak. I was silent. She caught her breath and gave me the details.

I handed the phone to Charles and collapsed into sobs. It felt like I was floating away with my father. Yet I could still smell the buttered popcorn on my fingers. I could hear the shrill cry of a woman asking her husband, "Where'd you park the car?" I sensed the frustration of an old man, bent over his walker, befuddled by the automated ticket machine. I felt the energy of a new crowd scurrying through the doors for the next show.

And it was Christmas.

Charles said, "Come on, let's get in the car and go home." He held my forearm and guided me through the parking lot. He buckled me in. I flashed back to those nights of shiny red noses and a snowman called Frosty and I cried for all that was gone.

Most people say it's coincidental that my father died on Christmas. I choose to believe he did so to memorialize the lessons he taught us on those Christmas light bus tours: Rules of social protocol are merely suggestions. Do not wait for permission to lead. And, regardless of religion, we are all more alike than we are different.

Those lessons proved prophetic and served me well.

23

Time Doesn't Always Heal

THE LIMOUSINE WAS waiting. I squeezed my husband's hand for strength—it was time. Dressed in an array of black suits and dresses, our family gathered to leave for the cemetery when my sister exclaimed, "Where's Mom?" I scanned our group. She was right, there was no sign of Mom.

"Mom, it's time to go," I yelled through the house. Silence. Louder, I yelled, "Mom!" No response.

Room by room I looked for her, as if trying to locate a misplaced cell phone. Finally, in the master bathroom, I eyed her sitting on the edge of her over-sized tub. Her wrinkled hand was softly stroking a CD player. Her eyes were closed, and her head was tilted upward. The slight curve of her lips made me think she was remembering the warmth of my father's embrace. Softly, she sang about memories.

I waited for the end of the song before jostling her into reality. She and my father had been married for sixty-three years, together for sixty-eight. Now she had to go to the funeral home, bend over the wooden box, kiss his lifeless lips, and grab our hands as he was lowered into the ground. Then, according to our custom, she would shovel the first spade of dirt onto his coffin and say goodbye.

I smiled thinking of one of my last phone calls with Dad. He was laughing so hard he had trouble getting the words out. "We went to that little Italian place and ordered a pizza. I told the waiter to cut it into ten slices instead of eight—because we were really hungry." Mom was giggling in the background. Together, they laughed effortlessly. Alone, there was no more funny.

Months later, I learned that time does not always heal. Things do not always get better. One can wither away from a broken heart.

Mom's old pleasures, like a sesame bagel covered with cream cheese and a fresh slice of sturgeon, the Miami Heat, *The Good Wife*, and mahjong were simply old pleasures. I tried to pull her above the swirling waters to no avail. Her grief was stronger than her grip.

Yet, I kept hoping. "Mom, I heard about a new movie that's supposed to be great." She'd flip her hand backwards, shake her head from side to side, and say, "Laura, today's just not a good day." Neither was the day before when she rejected my brother's dinner invitation, nor the day after (she had already cancelled breakfast with my sister).

Like the head of a tall man obstructing the movie screen, the loss of my father, coupled with her declining health, blocked her visions of happiness. She possessed neither the strength nor motivation to change seats or peek around for a glimpse of hope.

We had clung to the smallest signs of life. Like Fridays when she'd have her hair done, still in that early Jacqueline Kennedy style. Freshly coifed, sometimes we could cajole her to go to her clubhouse for dinner. She'd wear a Chico's print jacket over a black Lycra shell, accented with a splashy Swarovski necklace. Maybe vanity is the last to go.

We consulted those who were supposed to know how to make people happy. I sat next to my mother on the threadbare sofa at her psychiatrist's office. I learned about SSRIs (selective serotonin reuptake inhibitors); TCAs (tricyclics); MAO (monoamine oxidase inhibitors); and other antidepressants. We considered ECT (shock treatment) but ruled it out because of her age. As her anxiety escalated, we begged the doctor to up her Xanax allotment. Given her situation, what did it matter if she became addicted? Anything to quiet her demons. We hired a voice teacher who tried to distract her with Broadway tunes. A couple of times, Mom actually joined her in singing *Sunrise Sunset*. We hired social workers to help her talk through her grief. In the end, the best anyone could do was keep her mildly miserable.

When I'd wake up at 2 a.m., I'd fantasize saying, "Mom, it's ok—you do not have to linger. Go, go to Daddy." But how dare I? My pain from watching her grieve was no match for her pain from living without my father.

I was impotent. I could not bring her joy. I could not give her purpose. I could not pry her from her memories. No matter how much I wanted to give my mother the motivation to go on, it was out of my control.

I had to accept the situation. There was no other choice.

I met with my lawyer to rewrite my own medical directives and end of life instructions. I did not want to exist without joy.

AFTER DAD'S DEATH, we hired an aide to stay with my mother. She was not capable of living alone, and we thought that this was the best alternative. She needed assistance with bathing, driving, dressing, and other life functions.

We strived to keep her in her home, surrounded by her beloved artwork and familiar furnishings. It was only delaying the inevitable. I interviewed numerous candidates, checked references, and hired someone with strong nursing experience and a twinkle in her eye. I hoped that she could help lead my mother out of her depression.

I met them for breakfast at the neighborhood pancake house, which was one of Mom's safe places. Although I was twenty minutes early, I knew that they'd be waiting, and I was right. I spotted them in a corner booth. Mom sipped on an iced tea while her aide cut-up her waffle. As I approached their table, I became the child, still yearning for my mother's love and approval.

I pined for a loving embrace, a knowing smile, a spark of joy. A look or nod that said, "I see who you've become. I'm proud. I love you."

I got nothing.

I leaned forward to kiss my mother's cheek. She drew away from me, puckered her cheeks, put her hand to her lips, and blew me a kiss.

I choked back rejection. I reminded myself that my mother was afraid of getting sick. She wasn't avoiding me, just my germs.

And in that moment, I sprang back to life as the adult.

I slid into my side of the booth and skimmed the menu. I reminded myself that depression and aging had destroyed my mother's body and spirit. She had no hope for the future and little tolerance for the present. To survive, she divided her time into chewable parts: months into weeks; weeks into days; days into hours; and hours into minutes. She'd tiptoe into each fragmented timespan like a child entering a house of mirrors. Only, she couldn't find her way out of the maze. Each mirror reflected her plight.

She stopped noticing my children, my grandchildren, and me. We were obscured by the vastness of her suffering. She was unwilling or unable to strain her neck far enough to peer around the borders of her pain. A once vibrant, larger-than-life woman who had orchestrated galas attended by members of Congress, flown on the Concord, and achieved high roller status at multiple casinos was now a fear-riddled shell—playing her own records, listening to her own lyrics.

It was unbearable to watch as she drowned in despair. I didn't know how to save her. I felt like a lifeguard, trying to rescue a victim who had swallowed too much water. I pleaded with my mother to grab on and let me pull her to shore. I begged for her to surface, to provide a moment of respite, to breathe in the salty air, feel the breeze sweep through her hair, and listen to the cries of the seagulls.

But she had drifted too far out to sea.

I was jealous of her pain. It wrapped its fingers around her and kept my mother all to itself.

MOM HAD LIVED in her waterfront condo with my father for over thirty years. We emptied it in three days.

The day she fell in the shower, we knew it was time. We could no longer leave her at home with an aide. Her health had continued its decline and depression advanced in sync with her trembling hands, symptomatic of Parkinson's disease.

My sister and I returned to that senior living facility that my father had previously rejected. It was as lush as we had remembered, with a gym, pool, movie theater, and hair salon. The staff could oversee Mom's medicines, clean her unit, and assist her private aides with bathing.

Daily activities included field trips, book clubs, happy hours, and adult learning classes with topics like *"Movies that Changed Our Culture* "and *"Politics of the Middle East."* I fantasized about sitting next to my mother in theater-like chairs, glued to the words of the guest lecturer. Afterwards, we'd have lunch and reminisce about her long-ago trip to Israel.

In spite of the salesperson's warning, "Are you sure you want to commit to the exorbitant rent of a two bedroom? You know it's for you not for her," when a two-bedroom apartment became available, we grabbed it.

We hired a "specialist in downsizing" to assist us with the transition. She measured Mom's soon-to-be apartment to help us figure out what to take and what to leave. Then we met at my mother's condominium. An imported ceramic tiled mosaic set off its marbled floors. The walls were off-white, a neutral backdrop to accentuate her art. The fragrance of orchids seeped through the house. All that defined my mother—memories of my father, artifacts from travels, and her identity—resided in that house.

We agreed to move whatever furniture would fit into the new unit, then we sorted through her KPM porcelain plaques,

Lalique crystal, Waterford vases, Bing and Grondahl figurines, and Herand Rothschild plates. We stuck green post-it notes on her favorites for the movers to pack; yellow on the ones we wanted to think about; and red for what we'd sell, divide amongst ourselves, or give away. We wouldn't take much from the kitchen because meals were included in the monthly rent. The hardest chore was sifting through her toiletries and clothing. It felt too personal. I did not want to decide how many pairs of underwear and bras to pack and move.

MOVING MY MOTHER while she was in the depths of despair felt cruel and heartless. It reminded me of when I had to hold down my screaming baby at the doctor's office for a needle. Except then I was certain that it was for his own good and the sting only lasted a few seconds.

I wished I could be certain that we were doing what was best for Mom.

How would she survive in this new place without my father? She became anxious just trying a new restaurant. But what choice did we have? The fall in the shower made it clear that, even with an aide, she was no longer safe at home. My sister and brother considered moving her into their households. Their homes, however, had tight, walker-unfriendly corners, steps, and no space for my mother and an aide. I thought of bringing her to Baltimore with me, but she hated cold weather and how could I take away her last vestiges of familiarity? At least by keeping her close to home, she could retain the same doctors, hairdresser, and manicurist.

I swore that I would never put my children in this position. I would move before I was pushed out or make the necessary arrangements to stay in my home. But what if, like my mother, I lacked the capacity?

The moving advisor tried to conform the new space into a miniature version of the old. She placed the chairs next to the sofa in their original positions and the Lalique swan on its same glass coffee table. She had shelves erected for the other tchotchkes and hung her porcelain plaques in their previous groupings. There was no room for the dining room table and chairs but Mom had stopped entertaining years ago.

By the time they finished painting, it looked like a replica of her condo.

"Mom, what do you think?" I asked, as I held my breath.

She looked around her new abode, shrugged her shoulders and said, "What difference does it make?"

She never adjusted. She refused to socialize, eat her meals in the communal dining room, or go on field trips. We never attended any of those lectures together. Aside from a quick walk around the block, with an aide pushing her wheelchair, Mom quarantined in the apartment and stared at the TV.

She refused to engage with the present, and she didn't talk about the past. We had filled the second bedroom's walk-in closet with boxes of photos, a lifetime of memories shuffled together like a scrambled heap of playing cards. I pulled one out and showed it to her.

"Mom, look at this. Do you remember Danny's bar mitzvah? Wasn't your dress beautiful?"

She did not bite.

I second guessed every justification I had relied upon in building the case to move her out of her home. She would not have been safe in her home if she had stayed there. We could not count on outside help to cover all of her needs. Now, I wondered, was safety the goal? Would she have been better off with fewer days in her home than more days here?

Yet even though she was lost in her misery, she still would not allow me to sit on the white sofas or chairs.

"But, Mom, where should I sit?" I asked.

She pointed to the black Pleather bar stools we had bought on Amazon. They had small, hard seats and no backs.

I didn't argue. Discomfort mollifies guilt.

24

Happiness is a Choice, Not a Place

THE MORNING OF my father's unveiling, my mother said, "I don't feel good. I'm not going." It was already scheduled, and the rabbi was on her way. (It is customary in Judaism to have a brief ceremony in which the headstone of the deceased is revealed a year after his or her death.)

We held it without her. We promised my mother we'd perform another memorial service whenever she was ready. We did not want to push her for fear of triggering a deeper descent into depression.

Not long afterwards, while we were watching yet another rerun of *Ray Donovan,* my mother turned to me and said, "I'm thinking it's time to go and see Daddy."

Was she saying she wanted to go to the cemetery? Or was this her way of saying she was ready to die? She had been making comments like, "I can't go on like this." A couple of days earlier she had said, "I'm not going to be here much longer."

For a speck of a second, I felt relief. Then, like a snowflake on my tongue, shame melted the thought and replaced it with disgust. Was I really hoping that my mother would die? What was wrong with me?

"Mom," I said, "Do you mean seeing Daddy in heaven or going to the cemetery?"

Without hesitating, she said, "The cemetery."

The following week we hired a special transport van to take her to my father's gravesite. It was a production. The driver had to lower a ramp, wheel my mother into the back of the vehicle, and secure multiple straps to keep her steady.

All the while, my mother screamed, "I can't do this, I don't want to do this." Her aide gave her another Xanax. We assured her, "you'll be fine, it's only a twenty-minute drive." The aide climbed into the back of the van and held my mother's hand. The rest of us followed in our cars. When we arrived, the driver reversed the procedure. Once again, he lowered the ramp, unbuckled her straps, and wheeled my mother to my father's resting place.

I handed out copies of *The Mourner's Prayer* and, as per our tradition, we placed rocks on his gravestone. My husband began reciting the ancient prayer, *"Yitgadal v'yitkadash sh'meih raba."*

My mother interrupted, "I'm ready to go home. Now."

She never returned to visit my father.

"THE MOST POWERFUL hurricane on record in the open Atlantic region," warned a newscaster. Another claimed, "Seventy people already dead, over six million without electricity, and devastation approaching one hundred billion."

The morning after Hurricane Irma swept through South Florida a staffing coordinator from my mother's health care agency called me. I could hear her inhalation as she said, "Mrs. Black?"

I too took in a deep breath to steady myself for the news. "Yes?"

"I'm so sorry, but Tory just let us know she cannot get out of her house to take care of your mother today. Her street is flooded, and she can't get her car out."

My heart raced and sweat seeped from my armpits. "Can you find someone to cover for her?"

"We're trying. But, so far, no luck."

I panicked. The staff at her senior living community would check on her periodically but they could not provide the one-on-one care that she required.

I groveled. "Please, we've worked with your agency for a long time now. You know my mother can't be on her own. She's confined to a wheelchair, wears diapers, and needs to be fed and bathed. The aide with her now has to go home to help her own parents. I live in Baltimore and the Miami airport is shut down. I need your help."

She said she'd keep trying but I should reach out to other agencies.

I tried, but to no avail. In desperation, I called the aides directly. Six different women shared in my mother's care. I offered them bonuses, pleas, and promises. Finally, Sally agreed. She was not my mother's favorite, but she was an experienced and competent nurse.

The 30-minute drive took Sally four hours. When she called to let me know that she'd arrived, my mother shouted in the background, "Let me talk to my daughter. Now."

Sally put the phone on speaker. My mother said, "Laura, you know I don't like Sally. Send her home. I will not allow her to sleep in my apartment."

Mortified, I said, "Mom, you understand there is a hurricane, right? Sally risked her life to take care of you. She will stay there tonight. You can have her call me if there's a problem."

I was ashamed of my mother.

Not sure how to deal with this feeling, I began with rage.

My mother was always the sun. My father, my siblings, and I were the planets revolving around her every need. She was selfish and self-centered. She never gave me the stage. Her needs trumped mine. To further feed my fury, I began enumerating specific injustices from mundane to momentous: She never taught me how to shave my legs or tweeze my brows. She didn't teach me how to make a friend, neutralize angst, or bounce back from disappointment. Perhaps no one had taught her. She could not give what she had not received. That may have explained (but could not justify) not making me feel loved for who I was rather than how I looked.

I was on a roll. I thought back to my daughter's bat mitzvah. I tried to host a party that met my mother's standards: tablecloths from France, a band from DC, the freshest orchids, and prime cuts of beef. My mother came early to preview the room. As the caterers scurried about tending to last-minute touches, she said, "I can't believe no one has offered me an iced tea."

Like the heaviest set of barbells, I tried to lift my angst and focus on my daughter. But the weight of my mother's narcissism was too heavy to budge.

I yearned for a mother whose hug was so tight that it squeezed away my loneliness. One who listened to hear the feelings behind my words. Someone who swiped a stray hair from my forehead and dabbed frosting off my upper lip.

After my outrage dissipated, guilt moved in. I looked to excuse my mother's behavior. She had a history of illness, a childhood of neglect. My father had recently died. She was suffering from diminished cognition and loss of mobility.

But did this give her a pass from exercising empathy?

I thought about the time she taught me and my sister how to bake her apple cake. I could still hear her laughter at our inept attempts to sift the flour. I remembered how she taught us to understand value, how to differentiate polyester from silk, glass from crystal. And I remembered that when I was sick, whether with a cold or appendicitis, she'd call for hourly updates.

A couple of weeks before the hurricane, on one of my visits, we went down to the lobby for the 4:30 p.m. happy hour. A long-haired, mustached guitar player sang to the room filled with walkers, wheelchairs, and people like my mother, trying to escape from themselves. He began the set with "My Yiddishe Momme." My mother clapped her gnarled hands, knuckle to knuckle, in memory and recognition. Her voice was strong, as she sang along about "asking for forgiveness." *Was she asking me for forgiveness? And if so, would I grant it?*

AFTER THE HURRICANE swept through and it was safe to visit again, I flew down to Miami to check in on my mother. After greetings and air kisses from the seat of her wheelchair, she looked me up and down. She took in my hair, frizzy and unruly from the Miami humidity. I had not put on make-up, as I had rushed to see her first thing that morning. I wore capri leggings and a big work-out shirt that covered my body which I had kept to pleasantly plump. She continued to scrutinize me as if calculating my current weight.

Déjà vu. I was back to being the child told to stay home while the rest of my family went to that fancy client dinner.

I ran my hand through my hair and came back to the moment. My mother said, "I want to know how much I weigh. Do you think there's a way I can get on a scale in this wheelchair?"

Then it hit me. My mother and I had taken two different paths to the same destination. Mom the beauty route, her worth measured by her looks and ability to attract my father, a man who indulged her ravenous appetite for material consumption, parties, gambling, and a big life.

I did not possess her currency. Instead, I measured my worth on my ability to realize my own ambitions. I was blessed to find Charles, but we were partners with shared responsibility.

Brains versus beauty. Did it matter? Where was the line?

Separated by two decades, we were both fighting a silent desperation.

WHENEVER I VISITED my mother, I studied the other residents in her community as if they were paintings in an art museum. Harkening back to those long-ago residents from that nursing home, I sought seniors that would dispel my childhood image of aging. I looked for faces with full smiles, sounds of laughter, smells of perfume and body lotions, signs of optimism and fulfillment.

One afternoon, while walking by the gym, I observed a yoga class brimming with men and women who appeared to be in their eighties and nineties. I watched one of the participants, a petite Lululemon-clad lady who wore her hair in a bun, lean into a perfect downward dog. I strolled down the hall and stopped at a room filled with elders focused on a lecture about mid-century Italian art. Then I took the elevator to the main lobby where residents gathered in anticipation of the 4:30 p.m. happy hour. Bartenders cut limes into wedges and shook mixes of vodka and juices as they greeted the waiting drinkers by name.

A woman came up to me and stuck out her hand. "Hi, I'm Mary," she said with a broad smile and twinkle. "You can easily remember my name by thinking *Mary, Mary quite contrary.* Are you new here?" she asked.

"I'm waiting for my mother," I said. Then I couldn't resist telling her, "You have such a wonderful attitude. Are you happy at this place?"

"Oh, honey," she replied. "Haven't you learned yet? Happiness is a choice, not a place."

Her comment struck me hard. How could I age like Mary?

Once again, I reflected on the occupants of that nursing home from my childhood. These seniors were polar opposites. To be fair, many of the former had dementia and other life-altering illnesses that gave them little control over their disposition. But when we do have control, aging seemed not much different than any other phase of life. It came down to attitude.

Perhaps it was not a time to dread, but one to cherish.

I thought back to a recent family trip to the mountains. We had planned on going white-water rafting. However, when I read the brochure it said, "This is a level three rapids. It can be treacherous at times. Those with limitations, back problems, or other medical conditions should be advised."

If I fell into the waters, could I climb back into the raft?

I backed out.

"Oh, Mom, it will be fine. Come with us," my children pleaded.

It was so hard to say no.

But I was afraid.

I also remembered all the attractions I skipped at Disney World, opting to sit on a bench and wait for my family. And I remembered my chagrin when they raced to find me afterwards saying, "Mom, you should have gone, it was nothing."

Happiness is a choice, not a place.

25

Gut-Wrenching Decisions

DECADES BEFORE, MY father had sent me a handful of legal documents with a note that read, "put these in a safe place." They were titled: Health Care Directives, Living Wills, Durable Powers of Attorney, and Trust Agreements. They were unwanted reminders of my parents' mortality. One by one, I skimmed the documents. When I saw my name, I paused. My parents had appointed me their Power of Attorney, giving me the authority to make their life and death decisions. It made sense, as I am the eldest child and an attorney. Even so, I felt anointed. It turned out that the power was more of a burden than I could ever have imagined.

Gail had come to visit me in Baltimore. We were at dinner, sipping our wine, when my cell phone rang. It was my mother's aide.

"Mrs. Black?"

"Yes?"

"This is Angie. Please don't worry. But your mother's been lethargic and has stopped eating. I erred on the side of caution and called her doctor. He said to call an ambulance. We're at the hospital now. I will keep you posted."

Soon after, my mother's doctor called me. He had conferred with the emergency room physician. They suspected that my mother had a bowel blockage and admitted her for testing and observation. If their suspicions were true, she'd have surgery in the morning.

Between tears and fears, my sister and I spent the rest of dinner searching for flights to Miami. There weren't any that night, so we booked the first plane out the next morning.

When we arrived at the hospital, my mother was out of surgery and stable. But our relief was short-lived. Mom developed multiple infections and complications. Her kidneys began to shut down.

Each morning, I would drive from my hotel to the hospital hoping that my mother's kidneys had reversed their decline. Creatinine, a word I'd never heard of before her hospitalization, became a part of my daily vocabulary. It is an indicator of kidney function. My mother's normal level was 0.5; it was now 3.6.

A parade of "ologists" consulted on her case: urologists, cardiologists, nephrologists, neurologists, and others. None of them were optimistic. Eventually, her doctor took me aside and said, "We need to talk." He ushered me down the hall and into a legal-pad colored room, just big enough to hold a two-seat sofa, an armchair, and a wooden table. It smelled like antiseptic. I sat on the sofa, he sat across from me in the armchair.

In a matter-of-fact voice he said, "Are you her Power of Attorney?"

"Yes."

"Well, we can't find a DNR. You need to sign one. I'm sorry, but there is not much more we can do for your mother.

"There's nothing you can do?"

"She's eighty-five years old. She is not a candidate for dialysis. If she shuts down, it would be cruel to insert a feeding tube or keep her alive with artificial means."

He handed me a yellow paper to sign. In large caps it read, "DO NOT RESUSCITATE." I held it away from me, as if it were a loaded revolver.

"Okay, let me talk with my family. I'll get back to you in the morning."

I am not good at making irreversible decisions. I struggled with the decision to have my dog neutered. I didn't want to sign the DNR or agree to hospice. I did not want to play a role in my mother's death. Most of all, I didn't want to lose her.

I went back to her hospital room, kissed her, and said, "I love you. I'll be back tomorrow." Then I drove to my hotel room to reread those documents that my father had sent years ago. They were now downloaded onto my iPhone. This time, I read them as if my mother's life were at stake. The boilerplate language said:

"If at any time I am incapacitated, and I have an end-stage condition....and no reasonable medical probability of recovery...I direct that life prolonging procedures be withheld..."

Initially, I thought I was off the hook, that her directives were clear. It was my job to execute, not to decide. But I thought back to all the papers my businessman father had asked my mother to sign over the years. She never read them. He'd say, "Sign." She'd say, "Where?"

I also thought about my mother's fear of dying: If she sneezed in the morning, she called her doctor by the afternoon. She made an appointment for her flu shot before the vaccine was released. She wouldn't allow us to visit her if we had a cold. A headache was indicative of a brain tumor. Her favorite hand lotion was Purell.

Would she want to fight now?

In the past, I had tried to talk to my mother about her wishes. She never said, "let me die naturally." I pushed her, trying to avoid this very situation. "Mom, if the only way to live is with a feeding tube down your nose or in your stomach, do you want that?"

"OK fine. Do whatever you want. I'm not talking about it anymore."

Knowing that I had to get back to the doctor by morning, I stayed up most of that night talking with my family. Everyone agreed that Mom no longer had quality of life. Artificial interventions were more for us than for her. It was selfish to cause her more pain. If she died, who were we to play God and revive her? Fear of dying is different from choosing life.

The next morning, I went to the hospital with the signed, yellow DNR. But the decision was no longer in my hands. Mom's creatinine levels had dropped, her kidneys were improving. The potent antibiotics prescribed for her infections may have harmed her kidneys. The nephrologist changed medicines and she responded. Mom continued to make progress.

She spent a month in the hospital. I was there every day, although I never knew what I'd encounter. Like the time she looked at the rectangular device with the red call button that controlled the bed's positions and the TV, then looked at me and my sister and said, "I don't know what you kids paid for this remote control but it's the ugliest one I've ever seen."

We looked at one another, stifled a chuckle, and then she said, "Another thing, who picked out the furniture? It blends in with the cheapness of this room."

My sister jumped in, meaning she threw me under the bus. "Laura."

"Mom," I said, "You're not in a hotel you are in a hospital."

She shook her head and replied, "Well, whatever. And I hope you're not spending too much on the food. It's certainly not whoop-de-doo."

I turned on the TV and we watched *The Price is Right*.

I was way off guessing the cost of an all-expenses-paid trip to Hawaii when my mother informed me, "You know if I stay here, we need to take up all the floors and replace them with handmade Italian tiles."

Just then a hospital worker came in to clean the room. My mother was going full steam, "Ma'am, excuse me, you know it's better manners to empty the trash when I'm out of the room."

My sister and I wished that the worker took us away along with the garbage.

The nurse's aide came in to check her vitals. As she tightened the cuff to check my mother's blood pressure, Mom pointed to me and Gail and said, "Take theirs too and put it on my tab."

A couple of days later I arrived early enough to catch the neurologist. He asked, "Is she hallucinating?" I said I didn't think so. The minute he finished his examination and left, my mother said, "There's an elephant outside the window."

My siblings and I met with the hospice people before Mom's discharge. They educated us and made us question whether, given my mother's age and condition, it was fair to put her through any more hospitalizations. They explained that her doctor had signed their forms confirming that my mother had less than six months to live. If she survived longer than that, they would re-up for another six months and so on. They'd enhance the quality of the remainder of my mother's life with medication and therapy, including music therapy. If my mother went into distress, they would make sure she experienced a peaceful passing. If we changed our minds at any time, we could withdraw their services.

Mom's kidneys had stabilized, although her Parkinson's had progressed. While most of the time she was miserable, there were still sparks of joy. When she watched television shows like *America's Got Talent* and *Dancing with the Stars,* she seemed to sit-up a little straighter in her wheelchair and focus intently on the performers. Sometimes, she even smiled. Her face lit up when I visited—especially when I brought sesame bagels. And she still insisted that her jewelry match her outfits.

I played and replayed a video that my sister had texted me. On it, a hospice volunteer strums her guitar while singing to my mother. Mom cocks her head to the right and her eyes twinkle with recognition. Then, in a soft, compromised voice, my mother sings about beautiful mornings.

If I looked at the video too closely, I couldn't help but spot the emergency notebook lying on her kitchen counter. It held that yellow DNR. My signature was at the bottom. I prayed that I'd never have to make that call.

26

Briskets and Business

CHARLES CALLED ME from work and said, "Listen to this text."

He couldn't contain his excitement as he read, "Can you meet me for coffee or lunch one day next week? I want to ask you a question."

Feeling an adrenaline rush I asked, "Who's it from?"

"Lorin."

Lorin was my daughter's boyfriend. They had been dating for three and a half years. We adored him.

"So, when are you seeing him?"

"We're having lunch on Tuesday. Don't say a word to anyone, we have to keep this a secret."

I knew he was right, and with more will power than it took not to steal a French fry from my grandson's plate, I kept quiet and waited.

On Tuesday, as agreed, Charles and Lorin had lunch together. Later, Charles filled me in on the details and said that Lorin was going to propose to Jackie the following Wednesday at a restaurant near their home in DC. His eyes welled up as he muttered, "I bet he can't read Berenstain Bears to her in as good a voice as me."

The night of the planned proposal, Charles and I were too anxious to do anything but wait for Jackie's call. Their dinner reservation was for 7:30. By 8 p.m., I was pacing, cell phone in hand. At 8:30 Charles mumbled, "Obviously he's not doing it before dessert." At 9:15 he said, "I don't get it; what's taking him so long?" Finally, at 9:30 I got a text from Jackie. It was a picture of her hand donning a diamond ring. The message read, "I'll call you after dinner."

Incredulous, I called her and said, "After dinner! Are you kidding me!" She laughed, but took control. "Mom, he just this second proposed, let me call you when we're done."

The first person I wanted to tell was my mother. I yearned to hear her say, "Oh my God!! Oh, honey, I can't believe it! Jackie! Jackie's getting married. I love you. I'm so happy."

But when I called her, I got nothing. While it seemed that she understood that her granddaughter was getting married, she could not hold onto the thought. It hit me hard: she would never share my dreams of lace dresses and white rose bouquets. She wouldn't even ask about the ring. Two years ago, she would have insisted on pictures and a copy of the appraisal.

My mother had once set the penultimate standard for celebrations. Elegance, perfection, and grandiosity were her trademarks. My father used to love telling the story of when he and my mother shopped for my wedding cake. They drove a couple of hours for an appointment with the wedding cake king of South Florida. My mother interviewed him. "Show me a picture of the best cake you ever made," she said. The cake king's eyes sparkled. He climbed upon a stepstool and reached for a photo album on the top of his bookshelves. Filled with pride, he sat down beside my mother, turned to a bookmarked page, and said, "Look, my finest." My mother leaned over the page and examined the cake like she would have examined Jackie's diamond for flaws and said, "Can you do anything better?"

Without my mother to steer me, I turned to bridal magazines and surfed wedding websites. I didn't want to nudge Jackie. It was too soon. She deserved to savor her moment. However, a week or so later, the words thrust out from my mouth like a sneeze,

"Have you given any thought to where and when you want to get married?" I was gently chastised. "Mom, please. I will get there but give me some time."

From then on, I rationed my inquiries. In that space, tucked inside my mattress of joy, was a painful tick—another loss. Jackie's primary relationship was now with Lorin. I had been knocked down a notch. I would fill in some of that space by jumping deep into wedding fantasies. This gave me another, albeit short-term, diversion.

Alone with my magazine layouts, I envisioned Jackie descending a circular mahogany staircase. Her wedding guests, outfitted in tuxedos and ballgowns, standing around, agape, as she glided into a gold-leaf paneled ballroom adorned with massive Baccarat Crystal chandeliers. I organized a guest list and began searching for a gown.

A couple of weeks later, Jackie was ready to look at venues. Proud of my early surveillance efforts, I emailed her the links to my favorite ballrooms. She gave me the courtesy of perusing them before letting me know, "I think we want a warehouse. Something casual and fun."

I swallowed my disappointment and let it digest for a few days. Then, to my surprise, relief moved into its place. I remembered how I had felt like an imposter at my first wedding. I was embarrassed at the Versailles worthy wedding cake and the gaggles of wait-staff garbed in black-tie and white gloves. The orchestra was better suited for Carnegie Hall and the flowers for Butchart Gardens. As the lead player in Mom's pomposity, I had felt self-conscious and out of place.

I did not want this for Jackie. I wanted her to realize her own dreams. But at the same time, I felt traitorous because I felt like I was disregarding Mom's taste. Jackie understood. Like me, she wasn't ready to extricate her grandma's touch from her special day. Together, we found the sweet spot.

The wedding would take place neither at a fancy ballroom nor a rustic warehouse but at a reception hall on the Chesapeake

Bay with walls of glass that allow sunlight to flood the room.

Mom would not attend, but we would feel her presence. When I talked to the caterer, it was Mom who asked, "Is that the best cut of meat?" Likewise, it was Mom's voice that whispered, "Don't use their chairs, rent nicer ones." And Mom shook her head "no" to the standard tablecloths.

Mom would have been proud of her granddaughter. Jackie knew what she wanted and wasn't afraid to ask for it. She was comfortable setting boundaries and didn't allow the generations before her to steamroll over her wishes.

Always cognizant of my time away from my children because of work, I had monitored them for psychic marks or bruises in the same way I had looked for moles that changed shape or color. My concerns had been for naught. I took in this confident woman, my daughter, and I knew there wasn't anything better.

AS THE WEDDING plans ramped up, Jackie and I went shopping to buy a dress for her upcoming bridal shower. While I waited for her to come out of the dressing room and model top contenders, I flashed back to my own shower, over forty years earlier. I wore a denim jumpsuit, chunky heeled shoes, and an attitude.

To me, a shower was sexist; it made me feel like the "little woman." I resented the expectation that household duties were mine. I craved respect for my business acumen, not my pot roast. I envied the men, probably out drinking and partying. No vacuum cleaners nor dish towels for them!

Nevertheless, I did not want to hurt anyone's feelings. The shower organizers had spent time, energy, and money to plan this for me. So, I pasted a smile on my face, swept aside deception, and entered a living room brimming with chattering women and the aromas of yellow roses and white tulips.

After a proper period of schmoozing and indulging on mini tuna-fish and egg-salad sandwiches, blintz soufflés, and champagne punch, I was ushered into a blue velvet armchair. A ruffled, white umbrella dangled above my head. The guests arranged folding wooden chairs into a half circle around me.

An aunt handed me a present from the mountain of wedding-paper wrapped gifts. "Here, open this one and hand me the bow." She affixed the ribbon to a white paper plate, as I finessed a round object out of its square box.

"Oh, a crock pot! How great!" I said.

The aunt lit up. "You can put your brisket and potatoes in here before you go to work. When you get home, voila, dinner is ready."

I thought, "lucky me."

A cousin on my fiancée's side, pen in hand, was writing something on a legal pad. I asked, "What are you doing?" Snickers from the crowd. Then, a "you'll see."

I opened a set of knives, a paper towel holder, and a can opener. When I got to a matzah ball soup pot, I said, "Oh, this is great. It's so big." The guests erupted into laughter. More giggles and scribbles when I opened a set of sheets and said, "I love these, they're so soft, I'm tired of stiff ones."

It took me almost two hours to unwrap and fuss over each present. I could have finished in twenty minutes but I was admonished, "Please try and open the gifts gently, so as not to tear the beautiful paper." I guess someone wanted to reuse it.

By now, the paper plate was covered with bows and ribbons. Two ribbons hung, to make a hat. A gaggle of guests shouted, "Put it on. Put it on." I should have been a good sport and gone along with their request, but I wasn't.

The ladies refilled their punch glasses. It was time for the big reveal: The acting secretary, legal pad in hand, said, "now let's hear what Laura will say on her wedding night." Then, starting with, "It's so big," she read aloud my comments about the gifts, exaggerating sexual innuendos. I laughed along with the group. But, I thought, "When will this be over? Don't they know that my fiancé and I already live together?"

Now, four decades later, I wanted to slap my younger self. I had assumed that success in business required that I distance myself from the home. I was so driven to climb that corporate ladder that I stepped over traditions that would later serve to provide love, safety, comfort, and belonging.

I had distanced myself from the other women in the neighborhood. I'd watch out the windows as they swept porches and arranged Canasta games. I couldn't relate to them, I wanted more. There was never enough. I craved validation and hoarded successes. I had to keep climbing. I had to show that I mattered. I would do whatever it took to garner respect.

I rejected that which I could not achieve.

I didn't yet know that sitting around the family dinner table and asking, "How was your day?" would serve to ground me. I hadn't known that baking a brisket and potatoes in that crock pot would enable me to have those dinners. Briskets and business were not mutually exclusive. I didn't understand how a clean and organized home would give me a sense of control in a world where I had so little. I also didn't realize that household chores are not the innate purview of either partner. Like everything else in a marriage, they, too, are negotiable.

But my biggest miscalculation was the role that women would play in my life. I tried so hard to fit in to what was then considered a "man's world" that I had overlooked the ultimate power of deep and authentic connections with women.

It turned out that girlfriends, my sister, and other family members nurtured, supported, and loved me. They let me process, not just problem solve. They were not afraid to get dirty with emotions, share vulnerabilities, or shed pretenses of perfection. Some of the women who loved and supported me the most were hosting my daughter's bridal shower.

A close group of Jackie's friends and family were invited to her wedding shower. I hoped they'd skip the ribbon hat and refrain from predicting her wedding night dialogue. I knew they would embrace and help prepare her for this next stage of life.

My daughter's generation recognizes that women, whatever path we chose, are more alike than different. And regardless of our differences, we stand strong for one another.

I hoped that someone bought her a crock pot.

27

Just Like That

I FELT A heaviness in my stomach. It was not painful, just uncomfortable. I tried to ignore it. I didn't even mention it to Charles as I figured it was no big deal. It was probably just constipation or a looming UTI. I'd drink some water, maybe take Cipro. And I was afraid if he knew, he'd want to cancel our trip to New York to celebrate our anniversary and usher in the New Year with my closest friend, Susan.

During the almost four-hour drive, I shifted from side to side in the passenger's seat, trying to find a comfortable spot. We handed the car keys to the valet and checked into a small boutique hotel on the Upper West Side. I said to Charles, "I'm going to rest before we go out," and crawled into bed.

That night Charles and I met Susan for dinner at an Italian bistro just a few blocks from the hotel. I had no appetite, which was unusual for me. I played with the pappardelle on my plate and took a couple of sips of wine. Susan said, "Are you sure you're okay?"

I wasn't. I was exhausted. There was no way I was going to Times Square to wait for the ball to drop. I apologized to Susan, and Charles and I went back to the hotel. I climbed into bed, snuggled under the duvet, and fell asleep before 10 o'clock.

The following morning, I woke up still constipated, fatigued, and with a fever of 102. Charles insisted that we drive back home.

After tucking me into our bed, he went to a neighborhood

pharmacy and came back with an array of laxatives. I read the directions on the boxes. Their warnings read, "call your doctor if constipation is accompanied by fever."

I called.

I described my symptoms. He followed up with a couple of questions, then ordered, "You have to go to the emergency room. Which hospital would you prefer I call?"

"I don't want to go to the hospital," I said, "can't I try some medicine or go to an urgent care?"

"Laura, you cannot play around. You have to go now."

Charles drove me to the emergency room, where they were awaiting my arrival. After examinations, CT-scans, blood tests and more, the hospitalists said I had acute diverticulitis, something I'd heard of but never had experienced until now.

I was admitted and hooked up to an IV with fluids, given pain killers, and prescribed antibiotics. Everyone thought I was improving when, on the morning of the fourth day, Charles arrived early and leaned over to kiss me. His elbow swept my stomach and I shrieked. He reported this to the doctor, who ordered another scan.

My colon had perforated. I needed emergency surgery.

I remember Susan coming into the room and sitting on the side of my bed. We were alone. She looked me in the eyes and said, "Do you understand what is happening?" I understood. But the haze from the medicines and a protective layer of shock gave me distance and calm.

"Yes," I said, "there's no choice. If I don't have the surgery, I'll die."

When I woke up from the procedure there was a tube down my throat and I panicked. I gestured to Charles, my sister, and the doctor as if they were teammates in a game of charades. I brought my hands to my throat and pointed to my nose, trying to get them to understand. They didn't. My sister handed me a tablet and marker. I wrote, "Can't breathe."

They said, "You were intubated. This machine breathes for you. Just relax, the doctors said they'll take it out as soon as it's safe."

I fell back asleep. In and out of consciousness, I wondered why Andy had flown in from Florida to join Jackie and Danny at my bedside. Was I that sick?

I woke up again to Charles leaning over me for a kiss. I felt his tears touch my cheeks as he explained, "We've been terrified. You were septic. There was a problem with your lung. They didn't know if you'd pull through and told me to fly the family here to be with you. You're in the ICU. I love you."

This was too much to take in, I fell back asleep.

Every morning, Charles arrived at the hospital by 6 a.m. to talk with my doctors. Danny, Andy, Jackie, and other friends and family trickled in throughout the day. The doctors consistently said, "She's not yet out of the woods."

One of our rabbis came to check on me every day. I remember Charles taking my left hand in his, Jackie took my right. Danny, Andy, and the rabbi joined the circle along with whichever of my friends were there to form a circle of prayer.

After one week, Charles asked the doctor, "Do you think it's okay to send the kids home? They need to get back to work."

He said, "Not yet."

When I was finally conscious for long enough to comprehend, I understood that they had performed a colostomy. My surgeon diverted a part of my colon into an opening in my stomach.

I took in the swollen red hump, about the size of a golf ball, (a stoma) protruding a few inches to the left of my navel. A bag was glued around the stoma to capture waste.

I refused to look at it again.

After three weeks, I was discharged, armed with my new stoma supplies: rings, cement, powder, gloves, and disposable bags. Charles drove me home. The hospital had arranged for visiting nurses to stop in a couple of times a week to check my vitals, look for signs of infection, and glue a small, saucer-sized circle around my red lump, to which they attached a pouch.

Once, a few hours after the nurse left, the rubber ring peeled away from my skin—causing excrement to leak out. Never before, even as that fat child, had I felt such shame. But Charles said, "no big deal," helped clean me up, and reattached a new rubber apparatus.

Day by day I inched away from disgust and towards acceptance until one morning, as I stared up at the ceiling trying to make sense of it all, it hit me: Was this my punishment for judging my mother so harshly?

In order to process this thought, I had to unwrap a family secret. And in so doing, I was sharing the shame of another. I hesitated. It was far worse than sharing my own secret.

My mother had a colostomy when she was twenty-two years old, and it had never been reversed.

For most of her life, nobody knew about it except for my father.

My parents had told us that they relocated from New York to Miami not only for business opportunities, but because my mother was sick. She had uncontrollable ulcerative colitis. There was a doctor in Miami who could operate on her and save her life. Mom revered this surgeon but never alluded to the souvenir that he left her, a stoma that required her to capture and bag her own waste for the remainder of her life.

There were whispers and ambiguous references, like when she asked my father, "Al, did you order my supplies? When will they be here?" She never ate salads or vegetables, nothing that contained roughage, including her homemade, seven-layer, cream cheese-frosted carrot cake. When I'd ask her why, she'd say, "it's hard for me to digest." No other details were given, and I didn't pry. Whether in restaurants, theaters, or airplanes, she always insisted on sitting close to a restroom. Her pocketbook was heavy, and I learned later it was bulging with extra colostomy supplies.

All of that was unspoken yet formed a hazy picture much like clouds that resembled a face. I never asked for an explanation or confirmation; their avoidance of the subject made it clear that this topic was off-limits. In later years, when my mother began having issues with outdated equipment, she broke her vow of silence. She asked me and my sister to find her a colostomy nurse. In so doing, we, too, signed the contract of secrecy.

I hated that my mother was humiliated over that which she could not control. I wanted her to reframe her condition, to accept it, and to use her experience to empower others. Sitting on opposite sides of my parent's beige, leather kitchen booth, I said, "Mom, there is nothing to be ashamed about. You do not have to hide this. In fact, you could be a role model for so many others. You've lived a full life. You delivered three healthy children and traveled around the world. You even visited third-world countries with no toilet facilities and yet you managed."

"That's true," she said.

"How about if we explore some associations or foundations. If you wanted to, you could be a spokeswoman or a confidante."

She looked as if I had asked her to show me the device. "No, Laura. I'm not interested. Enough."

Recuperating in my bed while feeling my nightgown for telltale leakage, for the first time I felt my mother's shame. But I could not tell her. I could not apologize for my sanctimonious behavior. She did not know about my illness and surgery; she could not have handled it. She was already crumbling from the weight of her own declining health and the death of my father. I would not be the straw that broke her.

I needed her. I wanted her to swaddle me in motherly love. I wanted to ask her how she'd managed all those years. I wanted her to assure me, "It isn't so bad, you'll get used to it."

I thought back to my six-year-old self, watching as she put on that royal blue gown. Now I knew why she wore a girdle over thick panties—to hide the pouch.

Had she been consumed with her appearance to compensate for all that she couldn't control?

I'll never know.

Was my illness some kind of cosmic retribution? I don't think so, but perhaps it was, and certainly nobody can say for certain. The difference was that my colostomy would be reversed. It was temporary.

Just enough to give me a taste of my mother's life.

With my thumb and pointer finger I pulled back my nightgown, removed my panties, and looked at the stoma. Then I gingerly removed the soiled pouch and replaced it with a fresh one.

AS I CONTINUED to recover, I felt safe, cocooned in the warmth and love of friends and family. Charles barely left my side and my children spent as much time with me as their schedules allowed.

I was loved and valued. Content. I felt no need to justify my existence—to prove that I mattered. I was grateful that I had survived. I focused on my recovery, spending untold hours leaning over my walker as I shuffled through our condominium halls to rebuild my strength. Friends brought me dinner, and some even cooked for me at my home. Others sent flowers, books, magazines, and journals. I received phone calls, texts, and cards.

Wasn't this the feeling I had been searching for?

All of my life I had sought to be seen and judged worthy, first by my parents and later the rest of the world. When I achieved business success, I got that recognition, even glorification. When I stepped out of the ring, I assumed that, without more victories, I'd no longer matter. To fend off irrelevance and marginalization, I'd have to continue to produce.

Until now, I never understood that it was not about notching more triumphs, but rather accepting and relishing what I had already attained but took for granted—the love of family and friends. This is what filled that old well of insecurity.

I had tasted mortality and survived. It was time to live my life without judgment, especially self-judgment, and to replace it with gratitude and gentleness.

I had never been gentle with myself. It was time.

Before my illness, just the thought of day after day of unscheduled and unstructured hours would have exacerbated my post-retirement crisis. But now my perception of purpose unraveled. I had focused too much on producing and not enough on being. I was worried about filling my hours rather than the void that resided within.

In a strange way, being sick gave me the excuse I needed to rid myself of that frenetic angst. I could create my "to do lists" without judgment. If an activity brought joy, helped my recovery, or helped others, that was enough.

This "aha" moment called for practice and reiteration. It needed time to take root. Whenever I slipped into old thought patterns, I'd force myself to remember, *Time is indifferent as to how it is spent, whether with angst or gratitude, it marches forward. And it can end in a moment. Like a perforated colon that leaks poison into a body.*

BY SUMMER, I had healed enough to reverse the colostomy. But I wasn't sure I wanted to go through another surgery, hospitalization, and recuperation.

My body made the decision for me. I developed a hernia and it felt like a cantaloupe was protruding through my abdomen. Only my stretchy pants fit. The doctors could correct the hernia at the same time they did the colostomy reversal.

I thought about my mother and the opportunity that was never offered to her. What would her life have looked like if she never had to overcompensate for her shame? Would she have let down her guard and been vulnerable with me? Maybe she would have explained menstruation to me and helped me buy my first bra. She might have let friends drop by when her hair wasn't teased and styled. Perhaps she'd even go grocery shopping without first applying her makeup. Maybe she'd have been better equipped to tolerate imperfections in others, especially me, if she were not concealing her own.

As the September surgery date approached, my angst ballooned into a terror. I hated the thought of anesthesia, the loss of control. What if I developed an infection again or a clot? I read nightmarish stories of leakage and surgical mistakes. I thought back to my college roommate with the sign over her bed assuring her that God would not give her more than she could handle. How I wish I believed that!

I also thought about my paternal grandfather who had taught me all those lessons when I was a child visiting him in the back room of the gun store. He was the most religious member of my family. Brandished in my memory is the time I visited him in the ICU at a South Florida hospital. Failing from cardiac complications, he laid in his bed, tangled in wires, eyes closed, as if he were already gone. The visit had been awkward; he didn't have the wherewithal for conversation. I kissed his sallow, wrinkled cheek and picked up my purse to leave when I heard footsteps approaching from the hall. My grandfather became agitated and pointed to his yarmulke lying on the bedside table. It took me a few seconds to understand. I placed the skullcap on his bald scalp just as his rabbi entered the room.

My grandfather had displayed the enormity of his convictions by summoning the energy to show respect for his clergy. I was envious of his ironclad belief system.

Although I am proud and respectful of my Judaism, it was not tethered tightly. It fell short of providing comfort.

I turned to Charles.

He was supportive and said, "Whatever you want to do is fine, but why wouldn't you have the surgery?"

I wished I could handle stress like Charles. If it were him, he'd not think about it, he perfected the art of denial.

I thought back to our early dating days when I introduced him to my circle of friends.

Before going to my girlfriend's house for the big reveal, Charles and I had dinner together at a local ice cream parlor. As we ate our burgers and fries, my anxiety escalated. How would my friends react? They'd like Charles, he was funny, smart, charming, and disarming, but my ex-husband had been a part of their lives since childhood. Like replacing a cushy corduroy recliner with a sleek, gray, leather sofa, I was altering the chemistry of our group.

The waitress handed us dessert menus as I confided to Charles, "I'm really nervous. This is so weird. I've known these people through their friendships with my ex. They'll like you, but will they accept you?"

Contemplating the merits of a brownie sundae versus fudge-covered profiteroles, Charles paused and looked up from his menu. I held my breath, hoping for a whiff of wisdom, or an "it will be alright, I'll help you through this."

Instead I got, "What's your favorite flavor of ice cream?"

During our thirty years together, he has not changed. Like a lot of our male contemporaries, Charles still scurries from anything scary. He dilutes drama with a "no big deal." When my father died, while he was sympathetic, he reminded me that "every person on earth has to survive the loss of a parent." Another time, after a dinner party, when I regretted an inadvertent insult, he countered, "too late now."

I, on the other hand, became intimate with angst. I jumped into its arms and together we'd what if, analyze, obsess, process, and emote. When angst overwhelmed me, I ended our relationship with education, confrontation, medication, or meditation.

Out of desperation, I packed up my fears and moved into my husband's world of distraction and denial. It's where I needed to live as an antidote for emotional poison.

In the months leading up to the second surgery, I over-scheduled, over-planned, and over-stimulated. In addition to philanthropic commitments, writing, and spending time with family, I studied Hebrew and committed to becoming a B'nai Mitzvah. I planned a family trip to Disney World and hired a developer to create a new website. I downloaded dozens of movies and scores of books. I offered to host family birthdays and holidays. I socialized and discussed everything except that which was vying for control of my thoughts.

And it helped.

I had thought Charles' way of approaching stress was cheating, a copout. But I learned that sometimes it's easier to lose myself in an episode of *The Crown* than to focus on fighting the fear. I still had my other strategies. I walked on the treadmill, rode the recumbent, put in my earbuds for ten minutes of guided meditation, and ingested an occasional relaxer. I was okay.

Charles assured me the surgery would be "no big deal." When it was over, I planned to indulge in a bowl of my favorite ice cream, butter pecan.

28

No More Books

A FRONT DESK clerk ushered me along a wide, tiled hallway to my mother's apartment. I ran my fingers through my hair, reapplied my lipstick, and rang her doorbell. With a "Coming!" her aide Millie let me in and said, "Look who came here to see you from Baltimore!"

I froze.

My mother did not extend her arms for a hug or break into a grin. Rather, she sat slumped in her wheelchair with her head resting on a turquoise sweater-clad shoulder. Her fingers were gnarled into fists, prohibiting her from moving a mahjong tile or caressing the cheek of a grandchild. Her feet, once so sophisticated in Stuart Weitzman heels dyed the same color as her gown, dangled without purpose in Velcro-fastened black oxfords.

I thought about my last-minute grooming efforts and grieved for the mother who used to judge me.

I had recuperated in a haze of detachment. After a couple of weeks in the hospital and resting at home, I made a complete recovery. The fog dissipated and I focused my energies back onto my mother and planning Jackie's wedding.

My mother still did not know about my illness. Although we did tell her about Jackie's wedding, she couldn't retain the information. Yet she sensed that I had not visited her for a while. On our thrice daily phone calls she made comments like, "Are you in Miami? What time are you coming over?" I'd say, "Mom, I'll be there in a couple of weeks, and I'll call you again tonight."

My doctor had finally given me permission to fly, and, after three months, I was finally in Miami to see her.

I bent down to kiss her cheek.

She responded with, "I need Millie to change my diaper."

Millie wheeled my mother to the bedroom and maneuvered her into a Hoyer Lift, a full-length canvas sling attached to a hydraulic device. I was relieved that this time Mom didn't scream while swinging mid-air for the transfer.

When she was clean and back in her wheelchair, I suggested we go for a walk.

"I don't want to. Millie and I already went to the park."

There was no park.

I picked up the Daily Activity Bulletin. At 2 p.m. there was a jewelry designing class. She couldn't grasp the beads. At 3 p.m., there was a line dancing class, which was a definite no. There was Bingo at 8 p.m., but by then she'd be asleep.

My mother had not left her apartment for many months. Her doctor stopped to see her on Friday afternoons and her hairdresser came every other Wednesday. She was afraid to live and afraid to die. Her cries of loneliness and desperation undid me. "What am I going to do? You need to tell me what to do."

With the same voice I once used to convince my toddlers that there were no monsters under the bed, I tried to console her.

"Mom, you have three choices: One, you can try and make a life for yourself. You can go downstairs and watch a movie or invite a friend to join you in the dining room for dinner. Two, you can crawl in bed and decide you are done. Or, three, you can continue doing what you've been doing, staying in your apartment and feeling miserable."

Forty-five minutes later, I was back in my hotel room when she instructed Millie to get me on the phone. "I'm trying to think like you think. So, Millie took me for a walk around the block. We're back. What should I do now?"

"How about looking at your new mahjong card and asking Millie to push the tiles?"

"Laura, no," she said.

I didn't know what to tell her. I could no longer escape the truth. She looked to me, her eldest to say, "It's ok. It's enough. Go to Daddy." Sometimes, those words made it to the tip of my tongue, but I reeled them back in. I couldn't do it. So like a new pair of shoes, I kept trying them on, and hoped that eventually they would stop pinching.

"Mom, I'll call you tomorrow," I finally said.

Silence. I thought she had dropped the phone. Then in a voice so soft that I had to strain to hear her she asked, "What would you do if you had finished reading your book?"

"I'd get another book."

Her breath became labored and then she whispered, "What if there were no more books?"

My mother was only twenty years older than me.

THE DAY I went shopping for an outfit to wear to Jackie's wedding, my mother died.

Once again, I had flown to Miami to be with her. This time for her 86th birthday. I found her propped-up in her wheelchair, her gnarled fingers wrapped around washcloths, and she was staring at an old episode of *Dancing with the Stars*.

"Hi, Mom," I said as I bent over to kiss her.

Her eyes zoomed in on me and she smiled. But she could not finagle her arms into an embrace or lean forward to return my kiss. There was no "hello," "you're here," or "hi honey."

"So, how are you doing?"

She didn't respond, but shot me a look that said, "I spend my days in diapers alternating between the bed and the wheelchair, I can't feed myself, and I can't remember my caregivers' names. And you ask, 'how I'm doing?'—Really?" I felt embarrassed, like when I was an over-weight eight-year-old asking her for a second dessert.

"Mom, do you remember that Jackie's getting married soon?"

Nothing.

"What do you think I should wear to the wedding?"

Again, nothing.

For the next two days I sat with her but gave up on conversation. Instead, I resorted to a unilateral commentary about the dancers on TV. "Mom isn't she graceful? That's how you used to dance."

Nothing.

"So, who do you think will win?"

Silence.

On day three, I took a break from my vigil and went shopping with my sister for my wedding outfit. This was not an easy task. My arthritic knees ruled out shoes that hinted of fashion, so I needed a long dress or pants to hide my comfortable sandals. A bra was a must, so I couldn't choose strapless or one-shoulder gowns. I wasn't going to wear Spanx and similar fat hiders, so a dress that was stretchy and clingy were out. When I tried on those traditional, beaded, organza or other fancy dresses, I couldn't take them off fast enough. They felt like costumes, like I was trying to look like my mother, and I had no interest in playing that role. I wanted "funky" or "artsy" clothing.

I remembered how my mother dressed for my wedding. I had rolled my eyes when she bought silk fabric from Milan and commissioned a seamstress to design two gowns for her—one to wear and the other for a back-up.

As my sister and I pulled into the parking lot of the first store, I called to check on Mom. Her caregiver said she was congested, but not to worry. The hospice nurse had seen her and suggested Mucinex, and Mom had eaten a good breakfast.

Three boutiques later, still searching for that amorphous outfit, I stepped out of the dressing room and handed a navy-blue jumpsuit back to the saleswoman. Just as she was confirming that "it ran small," Mom's caregiver called me. She sounded flustered. "Your mother has declined in the past few hours. She is noticeably quiet and her blood pressure is low. I put her in bed with oxygen and asked the hospice nurse to come back."

When we got there, Mom was sleeping. My sister joined my brother on one side of her bed, I stood by the other. The room was silent, except for the gurgling sound of my mother's breath. The hospice nurse said, "She's in bad shape and having trouble breathing. I'd like to give her just a small amount of morphine, to make her comfortable."

I asked, "Are you sure it won't hurt her?"

"Yes, she's struggling. This will provide relief."

Not long after, the morphine did its trick and Mom's breathing quieted. Just as my own breathing subsided, the nurse whispered, "She's failing."

"What do you mean she's failing?"

I should have crawled into her bed and hugged her. I didn't know how. Mom had always veered away from physical affection. Instead, my tears flowed as I touched her cheek, stroked her arm, kissed her hand. I remembered the advice from those hospice pamphlets and said, "Mom, you've been an incredible mother (perhaps, a tiny exaggeration), I love you. It's okay, it's okay. You can go to Daddy. He's waiting."

And then the nurse said, "She's gone."

"She's gone?"

Wails.

Sobs.

Emptiness.

Finality.

Six weeks later, it was Mother's Day, a midpoint between Mom's death and Jackie's wedding. Grief took up most of the space, but I tried to chisel out a corner for joy.

I still didn't have anything to wear to the wedding.

I went to New York and consulted with a personal shopper. She asked what I was looking for and questioned, "Why the funky or artsy?" Her inquiry triggered a crack in my armor, and I knew the truth: in the past, when I had tried to emulate my mother's finesse and sophistication, I failed. To save my ego, I labeled Mom's emphasis on appearance as trite and superficial. I distanced myself from her values. She saw beauty, I saw ideas. Now I wondered, did we fully see one another?

I found an outfit: black pants with a print, silk cape. It was not what Mom would have chosen, but it would do. It no longer really mattered. Nothing fit right because a piece of my heart was gone.

I prayed that Jackie would cherish her day. I would be present for her, yet, at the same time, I would think of my mother. There was nothing I wouldn't have given to see her, in all her grace and glory, strutting down the aisle.

PART V

SAFE LANDING

29

The Wheel

THE MAGNETISM OF the ocean prevailed. I pulled the hood of my favorite green sweatshirt over my head to protect my ears from the wind and put my cell phone into a waterproof pouch that I tucked under my bra strap. A mountain of sand blocked my way to the sea. I reached out and touched it, the wet particles sticking to my fingers. Like an ancient sailor approaching new land, I sought a navigable passage. Eventually I came upon a path, a break in the sand wall, carved out by a previous adventurer. With a little finesse and exertion, I made it to the span of flat earth adjacent to the water.

It had been a cool November day, eight months after my mother's death. When I woke up that morning, I peeked out of the bedroom window and saw that, during the night, the sand had condensed into high mounds that had created a solid range. The formation extended both north and south, as far as I could see. It blocked access to my usual walking path along the water.

Tying my shoelaces, I reasoned that I could walk on the street, go to the gym, or just skip exercise all together. Back and forth I debated, frustrated at the obstacle in my daily routine's path. None of these options were as fulfilling as my beach walk. But my arthritic knees were limiting, and I could only manage flat surfaces. I gazed out the window one more time. I couldn't see past the sand mountains. In fact, they seemed to grow bigger and bigger. Was that in reality or in my mind? Did it matter? Aren't they one and the same?

I'm glad that I had decided to take the chance and climb the dunes to walk the beach. With every step, I felt free, unencumbered, and empowered. I forgot about purpose, meaning, and identity. Inhaling the salty air, I became one with I'm not sure what, but I felt secure and safe. As if I were encircled in Charles' arms under a down duvet.

I had almost abandoned that morning walk, allowing those mountainous illusions to block my path. How often had I bought into messaging supported by logic no stronger than sand?

I had told myself stories, bought into illusions, and, when left unexamined, such fictions morphed into truths. I thought back to my father's sign over that basket of batteries, "3 for $1.00," and the "SALE" sign that I had placed on the table of those pocketbooks. How easy perception becomes reality.

Perhaps my biggest misperception was my self-image growing up. After my mother's death, when we dispersed of her belongings, I went through those boxes of pictures piled high and stuffed into her closet.

I came upon childhood pictures. I ran my thumb over my five-year-old self. I was dressed in mismatched pants and top. I stood sandwiched between my paternal grandparents. Yes, I was chubby, but adorable with puffy cheeks, curly brown hair, and a wide-faced smile. In another picture, I posed in front of the Capitol with my brother and sister. My father had taken us to DC to tour the White House, Arlington Cemetery, and other historical sites. I was twelve-years old and wore a navy frock with brass buttons. I hid my frizzy hair under a partial wig (back then we called it a fall). The discrepancy between my self-perception then and reality were startling. Digging deeper through boxes and boxes of photographs magnified that twisted self-image, especially the photograph of me at my sister's wedding. I wore a low-cut, yellow, organza gown that stood out against my deep brown tan.

I looked sexy, almost pretty. Yes, I was still a bit overweight. I did not fit in with those rail-thin models with store-bought breasts and cheekbones. But, all in all, there had been nothing wrong with me. I only internalized messages of inadequacy.

To prove otherwise I had plowed my energy into business. From the time I was old enough to see over the cash register, I had worked at my father's store. I also sold holiday cards door to door and gave baton lesson to the kids in my neighborhood. Through high school and college, I worked a myriad of part-time jobs, including babysitting, preparing tax returns, and running a summer camp program. Later, I managed that chain of women's clothing stores and became a buyer. I went to law school with two children at home and a third on the way. I worked as an associate at a large law firm and, later, conceived of, built, operated, and sold the staffing business. For all of that, I had no regrets. What I did regret was holding on to the misconception that I had to keep proving my value.

AS I CONTINUED to walk, I thought about my parents. The longer they were gone, the less harshly I judged them. I focused on the good times I had with them rather than the disappointments. Like the fun we had partaking in the perks of Mom's high roller status in many different casinos. In Lake Tahoe, we slept in lavish suites. I bathed in an oversized tub that overlooked the deep blue waters of the lake. Snow-capped mountain peaks framed the background. In Atlantic City, I indulged in lobster and caviar dinners on fine china plates, which I discreetly flipped over to find markers of Rosenthal, Herend Rothschild, Christian Lacroix, and Versace.

I loved playing blackjack and memorized the rules, although the cards didn't always cooperate. I relished in the camaraderie around the table, the slaps on my back when I pulled an ace and jack together, the heart-stopping relief when I split sixes twice, doubled down, and the dealer busted, and the "way to go" from my fellow gamblers when I won the hand with a twelve. When I either lost too much or won so much that I didn't want to risk anymore, I'd leave the table and look for my mother. The flashing lights, bells and whistles, and roars of winners created a contagious, chaotic tumult as I weaved my way through baccarat and craps tables, roulette wheels, and poker games on my way to the high-level slots room. I'd find my mother perched on a stool playing The Wheel of Fortune or a similar slot game. Her walker was always parked within arm's reach. I'd pull a stool next to hers and join her in screaming, "Come on! Come on!" hoping to coax the arrow into landing on a jackpot.

I basked in Mom's elation, her eyes wide and her lips pursed in determination as she pushed the button and spun the arrow, pushed the button and spun the arrow again. I had been so self-righteous in assuming that I could do happy better than she could.

In that state of reverie, remembering those hours spent with my mother at the slot machines triggered an insight, a gift she never knew she gave to me.

What if I were to look at those pie-shaped slices of Mom's wheel as a metaphor, each symbolizing an area of my life: career, relationships, health, community, spirituality, learning, and leisure? Maybe I could simply expand the other six wedges so that they'd overflow into that seventh wedge, the one that had been occupied by work.

This interpretation gave me solace. It took away the pressure to find *the* replacement for my career. In fact, while I had been obsessively searching for that substitute, other parts of my life had already moved in and taken its place. I had been too immersed in the struggle to find purpose to realize that I was living my life to the fullest already.

It was time to take inventory of the remaining six sections of my wheel. I began with my health.

I had complied with the prophylactic advice of my doctors

and underwent mammograms, pap smears, annual physicals, and dental check-ups. Still, I had gotten sick. Once again, I had to accept what was not in my control but be proactive on the rest.

After a lifetime of struggling with my weight, I had learned that deprivation is fattening. When a food was eliminated from my diet, I'd crave it and binge. I no longer succumbed to that pattern. I ate healthy foods ninety percent of the time but allowed for periodic indulgences and wine with dinner. I had stopped chastising myself (most of the time) for not being skinny, but I'd continue to strive for a healthy lifestyle.

I'd incorporated exercise into my schedule, gravitating to activities that brought me pleasure, like walking on the beach and riding my bike. However, because of my knees, I was limited in what I could do. I gravitated to vacations that were marketed as "easy" rather than "challenging," such as bus tours around cities instead of hiking or climbing in and out of boats to explore Antarctica or the Galapagos. Despite cortisone shots, fillers, and physical therapy, I could not climb the stairs in my son and daughter-in-law's home in Delray Beach to admire their redecorated bedroom or the steps of my grandchildren's home in Baltimore to make a big deal over Connor's Pokémon collection arranged on his shelves and Zach's baseball cards that he had organized into albums.

I vowed to expand this slice of my life and scheduled a knee replacement.

The second section of my pie was community. I had held leadership roles in multiple organizations that promoted health care, education, and Jewish causes. My greatest passion was empowering women. I could ramp up my efforts by expanding my outreach through social media, my website, and marketing. Community involvement didn't need to be structured. It was oftentimes simply reaching out to the isolated or vulnerable with a note or a phone call.

The third fragment was spirituality. I'd never forget overhearing that girl in my college dorm complaining to her mother that I was "a Jew." Like my grandfather did with me, I wanted to instill awareness, pride, and understanding of Judaism in my children and grandchildren. To that end, we're planning a family trip to Israel. Last year, I became a b'nai mitzvah. When Addie received her bat mitzvah date, she humbled me into joining her. "Bubbie, is it true you've never been bat mitzvahed?" she asked.

"Yes. In my day, women were just starting to become bat mitzvahed," I said.

"So, let's do it together!"

I gave her a "we'll see," hoping that with time she'd change her mind. But she was steadfast and adamant. Her other grand-mother joined us. We learned our Hebrew letters, how to differen-tiate a dalet from a kaph, and basic prayers as well as memorized our Torah portions. The ceremony pivoted to virtual when the COVID-19 pandemic descended. Nevertheless, it was sacred and meaningful. When we visit Jerusalem, Addie and I will place our palms on the Wall as b'nai mitvahs.

I am also aware of my spirituality when surrounded by na-ture, like walking along the seashore or when I had agreed to go on my friend's boat and experienced the magnificence of the ponies from the sea. There are abundant opportunities to increase my exposure and awareness to the spiritual side of life. This, too, is part of the plan.

Learning was another piece of the pie. Here, there were limitless possibilities if I tapped into my curiosity. While I was growing the business, I directed my energy into planning my next moves. My interests were narrow: profit margins, entre-preneurship, retention, and client acquisition. Now, I had time to diversify. I liked visiting art museums; I could take a class on art appreciation or history. What inspired Van Gogh? What was Rothko communicating? I'd always been fascinated with psychol-ogy, and, again, I could deepen my understanding. What theories from my college classes are relevant today? Access to informa-tion was abundant. I could take advantage of podcasts, YouTube videos, blogs, and more. I could retrieve those catalogues from my file cabinet and look into classes at local colleges or virtually from most universities around the world. I could learn from those around me if I'd listen more intently and ask probing questions. I could allow myself to marvel at all that I had overlooked.

I lumped hobbies and fun into the leisure triangle of my wheel. I needed to give myself permission to be silly and spontaneous, and yes, to invite woo woos into my life. I had never learned how to "dance like no one was watching." Letting go was easiest with my children and grandchildren, like at a recent beach karaoke night. Each of my kids chose a song, stood in front of the TV, and belted out the lyrics. Capitulating to the chorus of "Bubbie it's your turn," I let loose with, *I Am Woman Hear Me Roar.* I needed to roar more often and let go of the professional persona that still lingered.

Like acting silly, hobbies were also challenging for me. I was never one to play golf, tennis, mahjong, or pickle ball. Although I did play bridge, I did so online. To that end, I googled ideas and scanned through lists of possible new hobbies that included stamp collecting, antiquing, bird watching, and so on. Nothing sparked my interest. I thought back to my childhood pleasures. What had brought joy without judgment?

My mother used to say, "Laura, please, put that book down and go outside and play." At the time, there was nothing I'd rather do than read. I loved the Beverly Cleary and Carolyn Haywood books. I'd curl up in my bed and delve into the antics of Beezus and Ramona and Betsy and Eddie. I also loved to write.

With a jar of Wite-Out on my desk, I'd sit at our family type-writer and spill out my pain:

I wish all the lonely people in the world
Could get together
And join hands
And share the mountains of unused love inside themselves with
    one another.

I also articulated a growing sense of injustice:

If only we were made inside out
We could be free of prejudices.

I thought back to that poem I wrote to my unborn child when I found out I was pregnant. Now, with a new urgency, I rifled through file folders, drawers, and albums. I discovered poetry that I'd written to my children for holidays, to my parents for celebrations, and to no one at all just to articulate my emotions. I also found speeches I had written to motivate employees for business and donors at non-profits, "We are more the same than we are different. We just want to matter. For women, whether by building companies or Lego houses, we strive to leave footprints that pave the way for future generations..."

Jumping on the suggestion of a friend, I signed up for a workshop on writing personal essays at a writer's center in Bethesda. On the first day, I left home with a protein bar and a to-go cup of coffee at 8:30 a.m. for the 10:30 class, allowing time for the stop-and-go commuter traffic on that stretch of I-95 that connects Baltimore to the Washington beltway. I arrived early with plenty of time to figure out parking, find the restrooms, and settle into my seat.

Twelve other writers ranging in age from twenty to ninety sat around a make-shift rectangular table. After introductions, the smiling, sixtyish female instructor gave us a prompt, something like, "write about an object that defined your childhood." We had five minutes to scribble our thoughts. The words poured from my pen onto an extra-long legal pad, and as directed, I did not stop to edit and filter.

We then went around the room, read our pieces out loud, and steadied ourselves for the feedback. "Sandwich your critique," the teacher ordered. "Start with the positive, put suggestions for improvement in the middle, and end on a high-note."

The writers were skilled and forthright. When my turn came, I thought about passing. But I steadied my nerves and read out loud an essay about the baton that had helped to reframe my identity from a twirler to a businesswoman. There was much room for improvement, but the teacher said, "You have a voice. You must keep writing." She ended the two-and-a-half-hour workshop saying, "It always amazes me how deep thinkers with interesting stories somehow find one another here."

I couldn't wait for the next class, and thereafter signed up for one workshop after another. I continued to draft essays on topics of interest to women: aging, death of parents, relationships, and identity. They were published in newspapers, blogs, and magazines. Encouraged by my readers, I gained steam and found that I was not alone in my later-life quest for purpose and meaning. I developed a website and posted insights. Many went viral like the one that reads, "When we embrace the emotions of change, we gain wisdom. It is wisdom that shields us and enables us to move on. We become stronger, resilient, and confident in our ability to withstand that which we cannot control."

AS I HAD experienced after my surgery, what held me up and pushed me forward were my family and friends, the final triangle for contemplation. I still had some emotional knots to unravel concerning my relationship with my parents, but I did not regret one moment that I spent with them in their final years.

Danny, Andy, and Jackie always were and always will be my everything. Work was never a rival, it simply bit into some of our time together. All three of them are married to extraordinary partners: Laura, Kristin, and Lorin. I've adjusted to the role of mother-in-law. I've tried to give them space to prioritize their marriages, waiting in the wings (most of the time) until I am needed. I limit my calls to them like I eat desserts: as much as I can without getting into trouble.

And it works.

Just recently Jackie called me and said, "Mom, I have a couple of weekends blocked off to bring my friends to the beach. Can we make sure the dates work for your schedule?"

The dates were fine. Then she tossed me the gift of saying, "My friends said that they hope you will be there, they love spending time with you. It's okay if you're not, but that's our preference."

"I'll be there."

During that beach weekend Jackie, her girlfriends, and I gathered around the gray granite kitchen island and played Taboo. When we were finished (I came in last), one of her friends said to me, "I can't wait for you to meet my boyfriend. I talk about you to him all of the time."

"You do," I said, "Why?"

"Because you are the only woman that I know who went all in on career and parenting. And you have excelled at both."

Validation.

Redemption.

When we went to Florida to visit Andy and Kristin, they cleared their calendars and made time for nightly dinners and daytime tours. Although we are separated by distance, they always show up when it's important. They make family a priority. Because they live locally, we see Danny and Laura weekly. They even asked us to join them for a weekend in Chicago. Although, in the beginning, I struggled with the guilt of not taking on more day-to-day responsibilities, that, too, resolved itself. I jumped into my Bubbie role, and the kids responded. Just the other day, Addie called me. "Hi Bubbie! Do you and Zaydie have plans for the weekend?"

"We're around," I said, "what's up?"

"You haven't met my new best friend. I'd like to bring her over to your house and we can all hang out."

"I'd love that," I said.

Later, my daughter-in-law called and added, "If it's okay, the boys want to come too."

Yes, it was okay. It was more than okay.

Despite the fact that my sister lives in Miami, we speak daily. She is my best friend, my confidante, and my hero. Along with her family and, sometimes, my brother and his family, we vacation together, celebrate the holidays, and are integral pieces in one another's lives. I am also blessed with extended family. I love both of my daughters-in-laws' parents, siblings, and the rest of the mishpacha. They have become my family too.

I look to my friendships with other women in a new light. When I was working, except for my few closest friends, I did not have the time to immerse myself into the nitty gritty of their lives. I also didn't pursue new relationships. It takes time to develop friendships, and since I now have that luxury, I've reached out and I'm forming deeper connections with a handful of extraordinary women. My best friend will always be Charles.

30

Labors of Love

LIKE THE KEEL of a sailboat, Charles has kept me steady through rogue waves of elation and despair. During a span of only five years, we dealt with the death of both of my parents, his mother's dementia, both of my surgeries, and Jackie's wedding.

He possessed the ability to keep his ego intact while schlepping with me to business conferences and charming my prospective clients. He held the ladder steady as I climbed up the rungs. He became accustomed to answering to Mr. Black (I'd kept my last name when we married) when we checked into hotels.

Then, in early March of 2020, came the COVID-19 pandemic.

While some still compared COVID to the flu, I pulled out the dozen protective masks in our storage locker left over from the 2002 SARS scare and I ordered gloves. I stocked up on hand sanitizer, anti-bacterial soaps, sprays, and cloths. I bought anything with the word "disinfectant" in its name. I filled our freezer with meat and chicken and the pantry with boxes of pastas, cans of tuna fish, and jars of peanut butter and jelly.

Charles bought Sauvignon Blanc for me, Johnny Walker Black for himself, and extra dog food for Einstein, just in case.

Considered vulnerable because of our age, we hunkered down in our Baltimore condo. I have never been domestic, but, like everyone else, I was soon scrubbing and sanitizing surfaces, starting with the toilet bowls. I polished wood floors with Bona, dusted glass tabletops with Windex, and washed the clothes and changed the linens. I disinfected faucets and doorknobs. I cut Challah into thick slices for grilled cheese sandwiches and peeled potatoes and carrots to accent roasted chicken. I made matzoh balls for Passover and a tenderloin for Father's Day.

But soon, the novelty of homemaking and sequestering wore off. I became frazzled and exhausted. The hot compresses that I used for my back and the anti-inflammatories I took for my knees no longer provided relief. It was time for Charles to jump in and take over, or at least carry some of the burden.

It turned out that, although Charles professed parity in the workplace, ovhe was content with inequality when it came to cleaning counter-tops and mopping floors. He'd rush out to the balcony for a cigar when I pulled out the rug cleaner or log on to his laptop when I announced, "We need to organize the pantry."

Charles was raised by a scholarly father and an indulgent, "do-it-all," stay-at-home mother. He has four sisters (he's the only son, the golden boy). Growing up, he'd debate political issues with his father while his mother and sisters set tables, lit grills, and poured drinks. Through our years together, he'd reluctantly hopped off of his entitled perch, but now he had reverted to old patterns.

Before the quarantine, allocation of domestic duties was never a cause for marital discord because neither of us did them. We were fortunate. When the children were younger and we were ensconced in our careers, we had the means to hire housekeepers, babysitters, and gardeners. As empty nesters we could afford to frequent neighborhood bistros and rely on cleaning services and carry-out. But because of the pandemic, like everyone else, we were forced to fend for ourselves.

As a couple accustomed to socializing and traveling, condo confinement was claustrophobic and challenging. Admittedly, it was harder for me than for Charles. He can sit in our white fabric, barrel chair reading historical fiction for inordinate lengths of time.

The ever-present stress of the virus took its toll on both of us. We feared for friends and loved ones, grieved for the loss of lives, worried about escalating unemployment, and stressed over contamination from those who refused to wear masks and distance themselves from others. It was not the time to fight. I did not want his laissez-fare attitude to trigger a "why do I have to do everything" meltdown.

Therefore, I kept it together when we ran out of chocolate milk and I offered, "You can mix Hershey's syrup with regular milk." He looked at me as if I had suggested dancing naked on a Zoom call.

When he bit into a burger and said, "Is this a turkey burger? You know I don't eat turkey," I fibbed and replied, "It's beef."

I held my breath as he took a bite saturated with catsup and mayonnaise. He didn't say a word but checked the label on the ground beef the next time I went to broil burgers.

There was the time when I surprised him with his favorite bagels and lox breakfast, delivered by a neighborhood deli and sanitized by me. He thanked me then studied the lox as if he were a gemologist differentiating a cubic zirconium from a diamond.

"What's the matter?" I asked.

Shaking his head, he said, "This looks like nova. I prefer belly lox."

He put his nose to the fish and inhaled. "It is nova. I knew it was nova."

I didn't tell him where he could shove his breakfast.

Instead, I exploded. "Who made you king? When are you going to help around here? It's time for you to be productive! This needs to be an equal partnership."

He looked up from his Kindle and said, "Well, if you want equality you have to stop doing so much."

I couldn't help myself and I laughed.

He added, "And are you insinuating that clipping my nails this morning wasn't productive?"

I shook my head. Against my will, my fury began to dissipate.

But I still managed to delineate a precise litany of complaints.

When my tirade softened, Charles conceded that he's not a self-starter when it comes to household chores and that, especially with food, he is set in his ways. Then he added, "Seriously. I don't need you to cater to me. I'm happy with frozen pizza. And there's lots of places around here that deliver. I can wash my own clothes, just not on your schedule. You can't sit still. You're always vacuuming or dusting. It's just the two of us, relax."

He was right.

It was for me, not for Charles.

It wasn't just to prove I could glaze a corned beef or clean a hard-to-reach corner with a toothbrush. To graduate from the pandemic with honors was my way of taking control. I was relying on old coping skills to get me through this new threat. It was what I had been doing my entire life.

Charles understood. That night he ordered Chinese food and, like the Charles I love, he bought enough spareribs, egg rolls, orange chicken, and beef chow fen to share with the staff in our building.

The next morning, when I came into the kitchen for my coffee, he said "I filled the Keurig canister with water, on my own."

When I stopped laughing, I said, "There is no one in the world I'd rather quarantine with."

Yet as the pandemic lingered on, forcing us together for twenty-four hours a day, seven days a week, without an end in sight, other issues surfaced. They seem stupid now but seemed monumental at the moment. Like when I asked him, "If you could go anywhere in the world where would you choose?"

He finished reading a page on his Kindle before looking up and saying, "Wherever you want."

"But where would *you* like to go?" I persisted.

Breathing in frustration and out exacerbation he said, "What does it matter? We're not going anywhere for a while."

I said, "Can't you ever just humor me? I'm craving conversation and you'd rather read your book." With that I stormed off to the bedroom.

Other times, for similar felonious offenses, I'd withdraw and regress into childish behaviors: I'd put on a TV show he disliked and raise the volume. I wouldn't forward him an article about an upcoming new restaurant. I mumbled "good night" back to him in a voice that was too soft for him to hear.

Ridiculous.

Was I a terrible wife?

With the same certitude I used to muster when starting Monday diets, I'd commit to stop reacting to insignificant infringements and cease passive-aggressive punishments. I messed up a lot. We both knew that my exaggerated emotions were because of the seemingly never-ending pandemic.

THE WEATHER TURNED frigid, and we could no longer eat or socialize outdoors. My claustrophobia from quarantine ballooned into cabin (more like chateau-sized) fever. I wanted to go to Florida to visit my brother, my sister, and their families, to see Andy and Kristin, and to go to the cemetery to see my parents. But we were afraid to fly until vaccinations were available and we were not a road-trip couple.

Charles hated driving with me. I held the steering wheel in a death grip, steeling myself for his admonition on my laissez-faire approach to how quickly we reach our destination. I winced when he'd say, "I can't believe you stopped at that light. It just started to turn yellow, you could easily have made it through."

"I didn't want to. I was fine relaxing for a moment at the red of the traffic light." I'd answer.

I gritted my teeth when he complained, "Why aren't you passing this guy? He's going fifty-four in a fifty-five."

I knew how to pass; I just didn't like to.

He usually drove, but it was worse when I was the passenger.

"Please slow down. We're not in a hurry," I'd plead to no avail.

He was always in a hurry.

Grasping my armrest, closing my eyes, and cringing, I had

gone so far as to picture my demise and Charles at the funeral finally remorseful for his aggressiveness. And me, looking down through the clouds, admonishing "I told you to slow down."

When we drove to the ocean for weekend getaways, we'd take separate cars. It wasn't fuel efficient but it saved on ulcers and blood pressure medicine.

I was about the journey; he was about the destination. He'd enter the addresses into both his car's navigation system and in the Waze app on his phone, to see which operating system won. If he inhaled the smell of a back-up or slowdown, he'd say in that frustrated and commanding voice, "Alternative routes." He'd change course for a two-minute difference.

He kept a running count of all the reckless jerks. "Did you see that guy! He just pulled out and changed lanes without even looking."

I didn't care. That was not the jerk I was concerned about.

As November turned into December, my itchiness ballooned. I either had to accept a COVID- and snow-trapped winter up north or withstand the trek with my husband. I waffled. Which would be worse?

That's when I had the idea of seeing a marriage counselor virtually.

The therapist sat behind a desk and peered at us through the computer screen. He was in his late sixties, medium built, dark-haired, and otherwise nondescript except for a piercing gaze that said, "don't bullshit me."

Charles and I, our chairs touching, stared back into the screen as he began.

"What brings you here?"

We filled him in on the driving issues.

After hearing us out he said, "It is up to the driver to make the passenger comfortable."

Charles rebutted, "But I never go more than ten miles over the speed limit."

"If it makes your wife uncomfortable, you need to slow down."

After a few sessions, Charles consented to drive "unreasonably slow and passive" to help me relax. In turn, I agreed to stop back seat driving and verbalizing excited utterances like, "Watch out!" I also learned how to compromise and adjust expectations.

Charles and I had a rich relationship. We both saw the humor in life and loved our friends and family. But by having the time to explore and delve into our habits, reactions, and motivations in therapy, we attained an even deeper level of intimacy. In so doing I filled in all the spaces of my wheel.

31

Last Remnants of Shame

CHARLES REMEMBERED THE location of their burial plots. He pulled his Highlander to the side of the road. When I saw my parents' last name inscribed in black font on a gray, knee-high, rectangular piece of granite I felt empty and gutted. On the left side of the monument was a Jewish star and my father's name, Allen. On the right, another star and my mother's name, Beatrice.

With the marriage counselor's words still reverberating in his head, Charles drove at the speed limit and didn't get (too) angry when I asked him to "slow down." We limited ourselves to five or six hours of driving a day. We drove south through Vero Beach, Delray, and Sunny Isles. When we arrived in Miami, we made our way to the cemetery.

As is customary in Judaism, Charles and I rustled through the nearby bushes and found rocks to place upon their graves. Struck by the stillness, I wondered, *what does it all even matter? Whatever our course, this is where we will end.*

It had been almost two years since my mother's death and five since my father's. Space gave me perspective. I wondered how much of my resentment towards my parents was defensive, a way for me to say goodbye, much like the way my children had behaved the year before they left home to go to college. Their kind, thoughtful personalities turned into snarky and remote personas. In so doing, they made it easier for me to let go. Had I indulged in some of the same distancing techniques?

I was next. My forever would take place underground. As with me and my parents, one day my children would use their bare hands to root for stones to place upon my grave. How would they judge me? Would they understand that they were always every-thing? That it was all for them except for that which I hoarded for myself—my work, my ocean.

Mothers mother the best that they can. We only know what we know.

My mother's beauty was her currency. It carried her from a childhood of desperation to the queen of her dreams. When she met my father, waiting on his table at an upstate New York diner, her life changed forever. Dad took in her vivacious laugh, thick ink-black hair, and sexy curves. He no longer cared about the food; he wanted this woman as his wife.

Mom wanted this same power for her daughters. When I veered from her script, she worried about my future. She could not conceive of a life without a man's financial support. How would her eldest daughter attract a proper suitor?

She did not understand that her expectations made me feel less than I was. They also propelled me to find worth in another way.

My father was smitten with my mother's beauty, her hurri-cane-force personality, and her passion. He wanted me to attract a man that would adore me in the same way he cherished my mother. He never contemplated that I'd find self-worth through a different path and through a man who loved and cherished me for my essence.

Unwittingly, Dad had prepared me for this path by sharing his wisdom and business acumen. I spent a childhood of Saturdays with him at his store, watching as he negotiated business deals, upgraded inventory systems, and motivated employees. I had emulated him rather than my mother and I hoped that had given him some consolation.

I began to cry. I had demanded that which they were unable to give me. I wanted my father to hug me and wrap his arm around me tightly, so I knew I'd always be safe. I wanted him to see that, although I didn't have my sister or mother's sexy physique, I had my own beauty that was simply buried within.

I wanted my mother to value the intangibles, those qualities that really mattered. I wanted her to teach me how to manage feelings and emotions, how to connect with others and be a friend, and how to age with optimism. I wanted her to live her later years without fear so that she was free to share her love with me.

Charles wrapped his arm around me and handed me a Kleenex. I gratefully accepted it and asked, "Would you mind leaving me here by myself for a little while?" He walked away, head bowed, and my tears came rushing out in full force, breaking through a fortress of misperceptions, yearning, and love.

I looked to the sky, caressed the cold gray stone, and said, "I love you. I miss you. Thank you. I'm sorry."

My shoulders relaxed, as if from the gentle pressure of my father's palm. My eyebrows unfurled, as if sensing my mother's lips on my forehead. My breath slackened as my lungs exhaled the final remnants of shame.

32

A Different Kind of Happy

FROM A BLUE-STRIPED cushioned rocker on my balcony, I gaze out towards the horizon at the majesty of the sea. I inhale the fresh air and take in the calls of the seagulls as they fly into formation. Sipping coffee from my mug that reads, "Hyphenated Non-Hyphenated Oh How Ironic," I smile.

It's been six months since I visited the cemetery and I've come to know that euphoric moments like this one sprinkle over days that are, more often than not, routine. Their presence, however, confirms the possibility that awe can sweep in at any moment if I stay open and receptive, if I am curious.

This bliss is deceptive. I have little control over it and cannot chase it. It comes from large efforts, like walking on the Great Wall in Beijing, and from small moments, like when my Cavachon, Einstein, crawls under the covers to snuggle with me. It's there when my grandchildren make me a card without an occasion, or when I'm home basking in the beauty of my mother's artwork that decorates my walls. And it appears when I put words together that elicit emotion.

I am aware of aging limitations. I reach out for Charles' arm for balance when trekking up the hill to my grandsons' baseball game. I break into a sweat when driving on unfamiliar, multi-lane highways. I'm excited by an Amazon delivery of bunion cushions and yellow-lined legal pads.

Pangs of emptiness and guilt still intrude on my contentment, but they are fleeting. As time goes on, their intensity has diminished. Most of the time, I am tethered without concrete measurements of productivity. I am enough. I am good enough. I am loved. At last, I have found a deeper kind of happy.

When I lost my parents, I lost the cushion between myself and my mortality. When I became septic, that morality became a reality. I was at the front of the line and the line was moving fast, too fast.

I continue to internalize what I'd learned from my illness. My goal is to cherish, not merely fill, whatever time is left and to plunge, full-bodied, into the wedges of my wheel.

When those drums of discontent reverberate within, I try to remember, *I do not need another ladder to ascend—but must relinquish the need to climb.*

Discussion Questions

1. What fueled your ambition?
   a. Did childhood messages play a part?
   b. Are those messages still relevant?

2. During your working and/or child raising years did you have hobbies?
   a. If so, do they still intrigue you?
   b. Name some new interests to consider investigating.

3. How do you define productivity?
   a. Are you open to tweaking your definition?

4. What were major times of transition in your life?
   a. What skills and techniques helped you manage?
   b. Can you tap into the past for strength in the future?

5. Do you have anything left to prove?
   a. If so, what?

6. What dreams are left to be fulfilled?

7. Describe a typical day.

   a.   Do you wish it was busier?

   b.   Is it meaningful?

8. Are you content with the quantity and quality of your friendships?

   a.   Would you like to add additional friends?

   b.   How will you go about this?

9. What are the compartments of your wheel?

   a.   What sections can you expand?

10. Define for yourself a "different kind of happy."

Acknowledgments

I AM DEEPLY grateful to my family, friends, and business partner for their unwavering support, advice, and encouragement. I want to also thank my editors Anne Dubuisson and Emily Rapp Black; my designer, Daniel Kohan, Sensical Design; and social media manager and marketer Meg Midwood, Digital Drip Media.